WHEN BAD THINGS HAPPEN
TO GOOD GOLFERS

WHEN BAD THINGS HAPPEN TO GOOD GOLFERS

Pro Golf's Greatest Disasters

Allan Zullo with Chris Rodell

**Andrews McMeel
Publishing**
Kansas City

www.andrewsmcmeel.com

98 99 00 01 BIN 10 9 8 7 6 5 4 3 2 1

Library of Congress Cataloging-in-Publication Data

Zullo, Allan.
     When bad things happen to good golfers : pro golf's greatest disasters / Allan Zullo with Chris Rodell.
          p.   cm.
     ISBN 0-8362-5216-0 (pb)
     1. Golf—Anecdotes.   I. Rodell, Chris.   II. Title.
GV967.Z85   1998
796.352—dc21   97-43231
                                                          CIP

To the founders of the Bad Golfers Association—John McMeel, John O'Day, Brad Lesher, and Pat Oliphant—with wishes that something good will one day happen to them on the golf course.

CONTENTS

ACKNOWLEDGMENTS

Thanks to all the pro golfers who graciously shared recollections of their worst moments on the course.

Much appreciated was the cooperation of the following: Jim Frank, editor of *Golf Magazine*, who granted permission to use excerpts from an interview with Greg Norman that appeared in the April 1997 issue; Mike Berardino, who granted permission to use excerpts from his article "Major Disasters," which appeared in the same issue; and Larry Guest, who granted permission to use excerpts from his book *Arnie: Inside the Legend* (Cumberland House Publishers).

A special thank-you also goes to Nancy Stulack, museum registrar for the USGA, for her fine research efforts.

FORE!THOUGHTS

Golf is so intriguing because no matter how badly you play, there are times—however rare—when your performance matches that of a great golfer's.

This doesn't mean you eagled the dogleg par five, or knocked in a fifty-foot birdie putt, or holed out from a greenside bunker. It means that every once in a while, the par-birdie-par pro looks exactly like you—the slice-your-drive weekend hacker. Golfing disasters happen to the best of them:

- Tiger Woods suffered two triple bogeys and a quadruple bogey at the 1997 British Open.
- Scott Hoch missed a thirty-inch putt that would have won the 1989 Masters.
- Ray Floyd rinsed a sleeve of golf balls on the finishing holes to blow the 1994 PGA Seniors' Championship.
- Hale Irwin whiffed a tap-in and lost the 1983 British Open by one stroke.

When Bad Things Happen to Good Golfers chronicles these and other outrageous misadventures endured by the greatest golfers in the world. The accounts are not written to poke fun at these stars. Rather, they are presented to ease our own self-consciousness on the links, to take heart that the pros feel our pain. They've been there, done that. Though this game humbles and humiliates us, it humbles and humiliates the biggest names in golf, too—just not as often. What separates us from them (besides talent) is that the pros know how to deal with a disaster *and* they learn from it. In fact, some of them share in this book the lessons they absorbed from their ignoble incidents.

To be honest, not all pros are eager to discuss their disasters. When Brad Faxon, winner of four PGA events, was asked to recall his worst hole for this book, he threw up his hands and declared, "You want to talk about what? No way! No way! I do a real good job of forgetting that stuff, and I don't need to be reminding myself of the disasters. I've had them, but I won't talk about them!"

Justin Leonard, 1997 British Open champion, says he puts memories of his bad shots in the bag with his club and urges us golfers to do the same thing. "In golf, the next shot could always be the best shot you've ever hit. Just forget about those bad holes or they'll eat you alive. Forget them."

But Arnold Palmer can't. Not when his worst hole has been commemorated with a bronze plaque for all the world to see. You'll find such a marker at the 508-yard, par-five ninth hole at Rancho Park Golf Course in Los Angeles, where Arnie once took an atrocious seven-over twelve. "That's one I'll never forget," says Palmer with a laugh. "That doggone plaque will be there long after I'm gone."

Arnie has been so endearing because he's won in spite of all the golf disasters he's suffered over the decades.

"You play this game long enough, and you'll do it all," says Hale Irwin. "And you can't laugh at anything anyone else does because either you've done it or you're going to do it."

Days after Ernie Els won the 1997 U.S. Open, he told Chris Rodell that failure is the nature of golf. "It seems like this game gives you more downs than ups," said Els. "I'm in my fourth year as a professional and I've played in probably sixty tournaments, yet I've won only five times. Just five. That's not very good, even though I'm considered one of the better players. Golf is a tough game, and it's going to make losers out of all of us."

His advice: "If you hit a bad shot, you can't let it rattle you. Don't second-guess the last shot—the one that hurt you. You're going to hit some bad shots, so accept it and think good things about the next shot. That's the only way to get over the bad shots we're all going to have."

Easier said than done, admits pro Frank Nobilo, who still shudders over the double bogey he took during the final round of the 1994 U.S. Open at Oakmont. "My worst hole, a nightmare," he says of the 425-yard, par-four third hole. It's famous for the eight grassy rows that run almost the width of a thirty-yard-wide fairway bunker on the left side known as the "Church Pews."

Although a double bogey doesn't seem all that disastrous, "It was to me," said Nobilo. "I had been leading the U.S. Open on the last day and that double bogey rattled me. I bogeyed the next three holes, and I was finished. The Church Pews did me in. Oakmont has the only church pews on earth where you go to cuss. Prayer won't help."

Amen.

WHEN BAD THINGS HAPPEN TO GOOD GOLFERS

Major Disasters

REVERSAL OF FORTUNE

Greg Norman
1996 Masters

No pro golfer has suffered more torturous losses at the brink of victory than Greg Norman.

At the 1986 PGA Championship, he watched helplessly as Bob Tway blasted his ball into the cup from a greenside bunker on the seventy-second hole to claim the title. A year later, at the Masters, Norman endured even more heartbreak when Larry Mize holed out a forty-yard chip to win in sudden death.

That should have been enough for any mortal to bear, but there was more torment to follow. He lost the 1990 Nestlé Invitational on Robert Gamez's winning last-hole 176-yard eagle. One month later, at the USF&G Classic, the Shark sank when David Frost belted his ball out of a bunker and into the cup for a tourney-winning birdie.

But nothing could compare to the agony Norman felt on the final day of the 1996 Masters.

During the first two rounds, he played with a calm resolve, carding sixty-three and sixty-nine to take a four-stroke lead over Nick Faldo. Greg played brilliantly despite extremely demanding conditions. Putts slid off concrete-hard greens, and windblown drives rattled in the pines. With the field stroke average soaring to 74.3, Norman was one of only seven golfers to shoot in the sixties.

"I'm very relaxed, very comfortable within myself," he told reporters after the second round. "I'm feeling good and looking forward to the weekend."

For the third round, Norman was paired with Faldo. The last time they had played together in a major championship was in 1990 at the British Open. In the third round back then, Norman blew up with a seventy-six while Faldo carded a sixty-seven and went on to win the championship.

Now they dueled at Augusta. After a sputtering start in which he bogeyed two of the first four holes, Norman settled down and played smart golf. He shot seventy-one to expand his lead to six strokes over Faldo.

Greg Norman's knees buckle when his desperate attempt at an eagle misses by inches on the fifteenth hole, sealing his doom.

Greg looked and played like a man of destiny, a man bound to win this elusive title. He figuratively had one hand on the Masters trophy—a replica of the manor clubhouse—and one arm in the green jacket. At thirteen-under 203, the forty-one-year-old Aussie was threatening all sorts of Masters records, including the then scoring mark of seventeen-under 271 held jointly by Raymond Floyd and Jack Nicklaus. He also had a chance to become the fifth player, and first in twenty years, to go wire to wire at Augusta.

It seemed impossible for him to lose. The biggest final-round lead ever blown at the Masters was by Ed Sneed, who squandered a five-shot advantage to Fuzzy Zoeller in 1979. Norman had a comfortable six-stroke margin, at the time the third largest third-round lead in Masters history.

Greg claimed he wasn't interested in any Augusta history lessons. After the third round, he told reporters, "Really, the only thing that matters is to play the last round just like I've played all the others."

For Norman this was the seventh time he was the leader going into the last day of a major. Up to now, he had won only one of those.

For the final round, Norman and Faldo were paired again. But unlike the day before, their Sunday battle turned into a replay of their 1990 duel at St. Andrews—with even more disastrous results for Greg.

He started off badly, pulling his first drive into the trees. It was a sign of things to come. After three rounds of sterling play, Norman hit just three of the first nine greens on the final day. He looked more like the golfer who had missed the cut at his previous two tournaments than the one who had tied a course record in the opening round. On the front nine of the final round, he bogeyed the first, fourth, and ninth holes and birdied only the second hole while Faldo nailed three birdies and suffered only one bogey.

At the turn, Greg's comfy six-stroke lead had shrunk to a nerve-racking two shots.

His downfall really began on the 435-yard, par-four ninth hole—the first of four straight bogeys for him and four straight pars for Faldo. Up by three at the ninth, Greg hit a sand wedge that spun off the green. A poor chip left him with a ten-foot putt for par, but he missed and had to tap in for a bogey.

Trouble built for the Shark on the 485-yard, par-four tenth hole. After his approach tailed left of the green, he sent an aggressive chip ten feet past the cup. But once again he missed his putt for par, leaving him only one stroke ahead.

He lost that advantage on the 455-yard, par-four eleventh hole. By now it was obvious that his putter was betraying him big-time. Norman missed a twenty-two-footer for birdie, hitting it about three feet past the cup. To his horror, his putt for par slid past the hole. He tapped it in, knowing his lead had vanished.

On the 155-yard, par-three twelfth hole, his seven iron hit the bank below the bunker. It was the same bank that had saved his faltering ball on Friday. But this was Sunday—and for Norman it was Black Sunday. The ball rolled off the bank and into Rae's Creek. After taking his drop, Greg hit a wedge about twelve feet from the cup. He two-putted for a double-bogey five. Suddenly, Greg trailed by two strokes.

Norman's only hope was to outmuscle Faldo on the two remaining par fives, the 485-yard thirteenth and five-hundred-yard fifteenth. But the two golfers birdied both holes and parred the fourteenth.

Still down by two with three holes to go, Norman needed a little luck. He got it—but it was all bad. On the 170-yard, par-three sixteenth hole, he hooked his six iron. And as the ball plunged into the water, so did the Shark's hopes of making a dramatic comeback. He took a double-bogey five and now trailed by four strokes.

The dazed, devastated golfer parred the last two holes, while Faldo capped a masterful round of sixty-seven with a birdie on the eighteenth. The winner finished the tournament at 276—twelve strokes under par—to claim his third Masters title.

Seconds after Faldo dropped his birdie putt on the final hole, the two competitors embraced.

"I didn't think it would end that way," said Faldo, who won the Masters in 1989 and 1990. "I came here hoping to have a good showing, not expecting to win. I just wanted to get a boost to the season. I honestly and genuinely feel sorry for Greg and what he's going through. He's a great man." As for Norman's disaster, the victor added, "It's part of golf."

By finishing second at seven-under 281, Greg suffered his most crushing defeat in a career that has seen many.

"For sheer gruesomeness, Norman's round of seventy-eight—a round that turned a six-stroke lead into a five-stroke loss—was truly frightful, like watching a head-on collision," wrote veteran golf writer Larry Dorman.

As always, Greg was gracious in defeat. "Nick played really good," said Norman. "I let it slip away. I put all the blame on myself. God, I'd like to be putting on that green jacket. But I'm not. And my life is going to continue.

"My thought pattern was good, but my rhythm was out of sync. I never felt tight at all—no tension in my body or in the way I was thinking. I just played horrible. I went out there thinking I had no lead, like the other days.

"Of course I'm disappointed. I didn't get the job done. I'm going to regret that I let another one slip away. But I'm not going to run around like Dennis Rodman and head-butt somebody. I just didn't win today. I'm not a loser."

A year after his Waterloo, Norman sat down with *Golf Magazine* editor-in-chief George Peper and talked about the most shocking collapse in major championship history.

Greg said that he relived his disastrous round about a dozen times. "But those were the dozen times that people have asked me questions about it. In my time alone—when I'm away from the world of golf, out fishing on a boat—I don't reflect on what happened at Augusta."

Norman admitted that when he thought he had control of his swing that day, he really didn't. "It was a gradual breakdown. Although I didn't sense it at the time, the first clue came at the tee of the fourth hole. I thought I'd selected the correct club—a four iron—and my swing felt just fine. But then the ball came up twelve feet short, in the bunker. When a player of my caliber misses his distance by twelve feet, something's wrong. My timing had gone off, and I didn't realize it.

"But the real warning signal came on the second shot at number eight. Again, it was a mentally correct decision because I had only 228 yards to the front edge and the flag was only about five yards into the green—a very unusual Sunday pin position. But I hooked my three wood and failed to capitalize on the hole.

"And what really told me that my swing was off was the approach to number nine. I hit what I thought was a perfect shot, and I came up three feet short, with a sand wedge—and that's like coming up twenty feet short. The ball landed on the brow of the bunker and spun back down the fairway."

Norman said he knew he had lost after walking off the fifteenth hole. "Until that point, I still thought I could win the tournament. I was just off the front of the green, lying two with a makable pitch shot for eagle. I put every ounce of my concentration and energy into that shot—mental, physical, visual—every bit of control I had in my system. I can still see the spot where I visualized landing the ball—and that's exactly where I landed it. I was sure the shot was going to drop, and when it didn't my whole body was just gone. Mentally and physically, I was just shot."

Norman said his collapse is "still something of a mystery" to him. "Never in my career have I experienced anything like what happened between the tenth and fifteenth holes of Augusta. I was totally out of control. And I couldn't understand it."

Before the round, Norman said, he was relaxed. "I was mentally sharp, physically calm. There was no hint of a problem. I even said to [his wife] Laura, 'Geez, I feel pretty good today.' There were the usual butterflies, but when I stepped to the first tee, I was fine. But as I walked through the back nine, I was in a complete twilight zone.

"I didn't know what to do. I knew the problem was in my swing, but I didn't know how to correct it. My swing had gone to a place I didn't know, and I couldn't retrieve it. Normally, I can make things work, I can manufacture the shots, even on a bad day. But not that day. At fourteen, where I had a simple cut shot to the green, I pulled it. I was out of control."

Norman denied that he played the final round too aggressively. He admitted, however, that his caddie, Tony Navarro, took the two iron out of Greg's hand for his second shot at the thirteenth. "He was right," said Norman. "That was a situation where I figured I had to try and make something happen. I'd just dumped it in the water at twelve, and I felt I needed to try to turn the boat around. In the end, I played conservatively and left myself a pitch of eighty-four yards, and then I couldn't even hit that shot properly—I hit it above the hole. So I guess you could go back and question whether the conservative play was right."

He said his debacle has taught him a great deal about fans. "I've developed a tremendous respect for the compassion of people out there. I've learned to be less cynical about the public. I always thought that if people read a negative article that had been written about me, they'd accept it as gospel. The response to what happened—the letters and faxes and telegrams—assured me that wasn't the case. It was like a big security blanket for me.

"I'll give you an example. I took [his son] Gregory to football practice where this man walked up to me with his son. He said, 'I've been meaning to write to you, but now I'm glad I didn't because I can tell you to your face. What you did at the Masters and how you handled it has changed my life and the way I handle things.' Here, I'd lost a tournament and yet changed someone's life."

The blowup also has altered the way Norman conducts himself in public. "I'm a little easier, a little more appreciative. I sign autographs on the course—I've said to hell with the PGA Tour rule of restricting autographs to limited areas. Bottom line, it has probably changed my life more than winning the Masters would have."

(The day before he arrived at Augusta the following year, Greg, seeking positive reinforcement, had a daylong session with motivational speaker Anthony Robbins. But it didn't do any good. Norman shot rounds of seventy-seven and seventy-four and missed the cut. Surprisingly, Faldo failed to make the cut, too.)

Gil Morgan
1992 U.S. Open

Gil Morgan knows painfully well how Greg Norman felt after the collapse. That's because few golfers have fallen so far so fast as Morgan did.

The nonpracticing forty-five-year-old optometrist wasn't given much of a chance to win the 1992 U.S. Open at Pebble Beach. But the twenty-year PGA Tour veteran upstaged his fellow competitors by shooting rounds of sixty-six and sixty-nine to go nine under and lead by three at the midway point.

When Morgan dropped a twenty-five-foot birdie putt at the third hole in the third round, he became the first player in Open history to reach ten under. His score dipped even lower, to twelve under, after he birdied the sixth and seventh holes. By then he enjoyed a whopping seven-stroke lead and it looked as if he would run away with the Open, the event's first wire to wire winner since Tony Jacklin did it in 1970.

But what happened next was one of the most dramatic free falls in Open history. "I kind of fell out of the sky," Morgan ruefully recalled. "It felt like my parachute had a hole in it."

Morgan double-bogeyed the eighth hole, bogeyed the ninth, double-bogeyed the tenth, bogeyed the eleventh and twelfth, parred the thirteenth, and double-bogeyed the fourteenth. By the time the hemorrhaging had stopped, Morgan had lost nine strokes to par in a span of seven holes. His once huge lead had shrunk to a single stroke.

He made a five-foot putt to save par on the fifteenth, birdied the sixteenth, bogeyed the seventeenth, and birdied the eighteenth to maintain his one-shot advantage.

In the interview room after his miserable round, Morgan displayed a little gallows humor when he told reporters, "All bow your heads. I feel pretty bad myself.

"It was a long day, and I'm glad it's over. It was kind of a dumb round and pretty embarrassing at times. Hopefully, this is my bad round of the tournament."

Unfortunately, it wasn't. After only a few holes in the final round, it was obvious Gil wouldn't hold on. He double-bogeyed the fourth and sixth holes and never recovered. He shot a bleak eighty-one and finished in a tie for thirteenth at 293, eight strokes behind winner Tom Kite.

Morgan had played the tournament's first forty-three holes in twelve under par and the last twenty-nine holes in seventeen over par. His final three nines: forty-one, forty-one, and forty. He never came close to winning another major again.

Later, Morgan couldn't quite identify what went wrong. "The pressure of being that far out front may have kept me uneasy," he recalled. "Maybe I was too relaxed. It seemed to drift away. I really don't understand that myself."

SPLASHDOWN!

Raymond Floyd
1994 PGA Seniors' Championship

Throughout his career Raymond Floyd has always been regarded as the front-runner's front-runner. Conventional wisdom says that if he takes the lead in a golf tournament it's a done deal.

But in the finishing holes of the 1994 PGA Seniors' Championship, Floyd shocked everyone—especially himself—when he pumped a sleeve of golf balls into the water at the fifteenth and seventeenth holes. Because of the triple splashdown, the holder of four major titles on the PGA Tour lost the lead and the tournament.

"I've been around this game long enough to know it [good play] can leave you just as quickly as it comes to you," Floyd said at the time.

Two weeks earlier, the fifty-one-year-old Floyd had won the Tradition, the senior circuit's first major of the season. Based on that performance, he was favored to win the fifty-fifth PGA Seniors' Championship at PGA National Golf Club in Palm Beach Gardens, Florida.

With three straight sixty-nines to open and an outward thirty-three in the final round, Floyd looked like a shoo-in for his second consecutive Seniors major title of the year. Although he never felt comfortable with his swing, the leader had built a four-stroke cushion over Lee Trevino at the turn on the Championship Course. Floyd—whose iron shots kept straying right, but not enough to get him in trouble—appeared headed for his fourth straight round in the sixties. Back in the media center, a Senior PGA Tour official was preparing a highlight sheet headlined "Raymond Floyd—With His Victory Today . . ."

But the highlight sheet had to be scrapped. Floyd bogeyed the eleventh hole when he failed to make a sand save while Trevino birdied the tenth and thirteenth. Floyd's lead had been shaved to one stroke as the playing partners entered "The Bear Trap"—four finishing holes guarded by water.

At the 164-yard, par-three fifteenth, they played into the wind. Because of the breeze, golfers were aiming at bunkers or the water, hoping the wind would push their balls onto the green. That's what Trevino did, hitting safely to the left side of the green.

Ray Floyd hits his tee shot on the fifteenth hole into the water (top left), grimaces before rinsing his next try (above), and then glumly takes a drop (bottom left).

Now it was Floyd's turn. The water hole had claimed his tee shot two days earlier as it had a dozen others throughout the tournament. But on Sunday Floyd blocked all that from his mind. Unfortunately, what he also blocked was his five-iron tee shot. The ball sailed right and plunked into the water. From the drop zone, the miffed golfer sent his six iron over the green—and into the lily-pad-covered pond on the other side. After another drop, he chipped from behind the green to within six feet of the cup, and then missed the putt. He walked off with a stunning quadruple-bogey seven to Trevino's par. Floyd's disaster was a four-stroke turnaround. Up by one, he now trailed by three.

Recalled Trevino, "I had to really compose myself going to the sixteenth tee. It's crazy when you're a shot back and all of a sudden you're three up. That doesn't happen very often. If you know Raymond Floyd, you know that nobody manages a golf course better than he does."

But if Floyd was rattled, he didn't show it at the sixteenth. He banged in a forty-foot birdie putt and picked up a stroke on Trevino.

But any chance to catch the leader was drenched at the 152-yard, par-three seventeenth. To his dismay, Floyd watched his seven-iron tee shot soar right and plunge into the water again. After a drop, he hit a nine iron to within twenty feet and two-putted for a double-bogey five. He parred the final hole.

Trevino parred the sixteenth and seventeenth and three-putted the eighteenth from fifty feet for a closing round of seventy. His nine-under 279 total was one stroke better than runner-up Jim Colbert. Floyd shot a woeful seventy-five—forty-two on the back, nine shots worse than the front—and tied Dave Stockton for third place with 282.

As Floyd's caddie walked out of the scoring tent beside the last hole, a youngster asked for a ball to keep as a souvenir. "We left them all in the water," the caddie said with a cynical smile. "We've got none left."

After the victory, Trevino told reporters, "I was as shocked as Raymond was. He gave it to me on a silver platter. Raymond was Santa Claus."

Floyd didn't discount Trevino's effort, but he took the blame for the loss. "I was getting the job done. Then I hit the ball into the water. What can you say? I did the damage. He didn't."

The friendly rivalry between the two goes back to 1965, when, as both men tell the tale, Trevino was hustling at the Horizon Hills Country Club in El Paso, Texas. A hotshot Tour player named Raymond Floyd was brought in to duel a local favorite bankrolled by cotton farmers. Floyd drove up in a white Cadillac and was met by a Mexican who took the pro's clubs out of the trunk, showed him to a locker, and even cleaned his shoes. "Who am I playing today?" Floyd asked. Replied the Mexican, "You're talking to him."

Floyd lost the first two rounds to the "clubhouse boy" but saved face by eagling the eighteenth to beat Trevino by a shot in their third round.

Floyd then left El Paso, saying, "I've got easier games than this on the Tour."

Floyd knows tournament golf isn't that easy. He confessed to reporters that the pressure at the Seniors' Championship got to him. "I had been playing beautifully all week, for the last three or four weeks," he said after the loss. "I have to put the onus on the pressure. It seemed every iron I hit today and most tee shots went right."

He called the two par threes in the Bear Trap "the hardest I've ever seen to put the ball on the green" because the greens are so narrow. "I'd hate to have to play those holes day in and day out for a lot of money. My hair would really be gray."

He said the defeat didn't hurt as much as his Masters loss to Nick Faldo in 1990. That year, Floyd had a one-stroke lead after seventy holes, but three-putted for bogey at the seventeenth, causing a play-off. Then he pulled a seven iron into the water at the eleventh to lose on the second play-off hole.

If the Seniors' Championship tailspin pained him, it was in the wallet. Each one of those water balls cost Floyd $19,166.67—the difference between $115,000 for first and $57,500 for a third-place tie.

"Do I act devastated? I'm not. It's a golf tournament," he added with a shrug. "To be honest, I look at it as a learning experience."

He finally figured out why, under certain circumstances, he was hitting the ball to the right. "I think under pressure I stand too close to the ball. That makes me push the ball out to the right. I fell out of the proper ball position and couldn't release. Maybe I got a little out of my routine. Maybe I wasn't thinking clearly."

Not until the seventeenth hole did he realize what he was doing wrong: "When I dropped the ball [after he rinsed his tee shot] something inside me said, 'You're too close to the ball.' I backed up slightly and made my first free swing of the day. I'm going to take this loss as a positive. All I ask for is the opportunity to put myself in a position to win again. I hope I don't blow an engine like I did today."

Apparently, he learned his lesson well. In his next tournament, the Las Vegas Senior Classic, Floyd won by three strokes over his nearest competitor.

But the real test came the following year at the PGA Seniors' Championship at PGA National. As he had in 1994, Floyd held a seemingly comfortable lead at the turn in the final round. This time, he had a five-stroke margin. No way was he going to wet another sleeve of balls in the Bear Trap.

At the par-three fifteenth, Floyd took a seven iron and aimed at a palm tree behind the green. He refused to give any thought to last year's water troubles. "You've got to put those things in the past," he said later. "And I did."

This time, his ball landed safely on the left front of the green. Floyd two-putted for his par. He did the same thing at the seventeenth and maintained his five-stroke edge to seize the title he had blown in 1994. Three players, one of them Trevino, finished in a tie for second.

Floyd shot an eleven-under 277, making par on the fifteenth and seventeenth holes in all four rounds. But he wasn't boasting about getting his revenge on the course. "Believe me," he said recently, "I've played enough golf courses, tournaments, and holes that have whipped me. If I had to try to get even, there wouldn't be enough time in my life."

Today, Floyd thinks that one of the keys to his success is his ability to learn from failure. And he credits his wife, Maria, for helping him appreciate the importance of analyzing his mistakes.

The turning point in his golfing philosophy occurred in 1986 after he blew a lead in the last round of the Westchester Classic by shooting a horrendous seventy-seven. The timing couldn't have been worse because it was the final tuneup for the U.S. Open at Shinnecock Hills.

During the tense car ride from Rye, New York, to Southampton, Long Island, with Maria, he wanted to forget about his Westchester outing. She didn't.

"I was pretty much the kind of person who will sweep it under the rug and let it go if bad things happen," he recalled. "But Maria likes to address things, and the crux of the whole conversation was, 'If you get in contention for the U.S. Open this Sunday, you better think about what happened today because it might happen again.'"

Floyd said he eventually opened up and went over each mistake. "I either had to give in to Maria, get a divorce, or I had to put her out on the road," said Floyd. "But you know how wives generally win, anyway. I addressed it [his Westchester blowup], and thank goodness I did because you have got to learn from your mistakes. It's a learning process whether you win, lose, or draw, but it is something I was not ready to face, and I'm glad she forced me into doing that."

The following week, Floyd won the U.S. Open.

Jack Nicklaus
1976 Bing Crosby National Pro-Am

Jack Nicklaus knows all about the dangers of the Bear Trap on PGA National's Championship Course. He's the one who redesigned it in 1990, molding the last four holes into an unforgiving watery grave for all those mis-hit balls.

Ironically, the Bear Trap snared the Bear himself in the first round of the 1994 PGA Seniors' Championship. He hit into the water on both the fifteenth and seventeenth holes and made bogey on each one. The following year, Nicklaus tried to make a run on Floyd in the final round. Jack started the day in third place, only three shots behind. But he got caught in the Bear Trap and bogeyed the fifteenth, sixteenth, and seventeenth to shoot seventy-four and finish eighth.

As embarrassing as that was for Nicklaus, he was mortified by his misfortune on his favorite golf course—Pebble Beach. In the final round of the 1976 Bing Crosby National Pro-Am, Jack shot a startling eighty-two. He played the back nine in nine-over forty-five—that's even-bogey golf!

Nicklaus entered the final day hanging on to a three-stroke lead at 209. But he shot a one-over thirty-seven on the front nine and dropped behind new leader Mike Morley by a stroke. Jack remained in contention until the par-four thirteenth hole. From a perfect position in the fairway, he hit a horrible hook that ended up on hardpan near the road that paralleled the hole. Jack tried to roll the ball over the mound that protected the green, but he didn't quite make it and the ball rolled back to him. He took a double-bogey six and suffered two more bogeys. Then it got worse.

On the par-three seventeenth, which he had birdied the day before, Nicklaus buried his tee shot in the front bunker. His explosion shot was a dud, moving the ball only a foot, into a crevice. Recalled Jack, "Hoagy [Bob Hoag, his amateur playing partner] started laughing, so I did, too. The whole thing became comical." Jack took a double-bogey five.

Now on a slippery slide toward oblivion, Nicklaus didn't stand a chance of duplicating the birdie he made on the par-five eighteenth the day before. A flubbed approach and lousy putting led to a triple-bogey eight. He staggered off the course with one of the worst rounds of his magnificent career. He had plunged from a tie for second place to a tie for eighteenth.

"Fortunately, those kind of things didn't happen to me very often, but they have happened," he said recently. "What can you do about it? Nothing except get ready for the next tournament."

A FAILURE TO COMMUNICATE

Sam Snead
1939 U.S. Open

Sam Snead racked up eighty-one PGA Tour victories and won at least another eighty events. He's a four-time Vardon Trophy winner and a member of eight Ryder Cup teams and three World Cup squads. He's also a member of the PGA and World Golf Halls of Fame.

But for all his accomplishments, there still remains one regret—his failure to win the 1939 U.S. Open. He had the title in his back pocket but let it get picked, all because of a simple communication problem. Many years later, Snead would refer to it as "one of the biggest blowups in the history of golf." With a touch of hyperbole, he added, "This blowup was so big pieces of me were still coming down a week later."

The twenty-seven-year-old Hot Springs, Virginia, native had quickly captured the golf world's attention with his majestic swing and mountain twang. He surprised everyone by finishing second, two strokes behind winner Ralph Guldahl, in the 1937 U.S. Open at Oakland Hills Country Club near Detroit. The following year, Slammin' Sam won eight Tour events and was the leading money winner.

He started the 1939 season by recording three wins and a second at the Masters (won by Guldahl). By the time of the U.S. Open, at Philadelphia Country Club's Spring Mill layout, Snead was primed for victory. He fired rounds of sixty-eight, seventy-one, and seventy-three and entered the final day one stroke behind his friend Johnny Bulla.

By the seventeenth hole, Snead had taken the lead. If he parred both holes, he would finish with a seventy and a 282 total. But he had no clue whether that number was good enough to win.

With today's computerized scoreboards, a player can know where he stands at all times. But back then there was no such information readily available to the golfers, who marked their own cards and then double-checked at the end of each round to make sure the scoring was accurate. Recalled Snead, "I knew exactly where I stood, but I had only a fuzzy notion of what the other fellas were doing."

Snead's big mistake was that he never bothered to ask.

Mistakenly thinking he must birdie the final hole when a par would win the 1939 U.S. Open, Sam Snead hooks his drive—and winds up with a shocking triple bogey.

He assumed he had to beat Johnny Bulla or Byron Nelson. Bulla fell out of contention. What Snead didn't know was that Nelson, who had played ahead of Sam, had finished at 284. That meant Snead could coast to his first major title. "If I'd known that was his score, I'd have taken life a little easier on the last two holes," Snead recalled in his autobiography *Slammin' Sam*. "As it was, I was so scared of blowing the Open I decided to go all out."

On the par-four seventeenth, his approach landed in the rough. He chipped way short of the pin and two-putted for a bogey five. That made Sam sweat even more as he headed for the 558-yard, par-five eighteenth. In his favor, it was an easy par five that many golfers in the tourney had birdied.

As Snead prepared to tee off, most spectators knew a par would beat Nelson's 284. But to his everlasting regret, Snead figured he needed to birdie the hole.

"I wish I'd known there was no need to sweat," he recalled. "Trouble is, those coming back from the clubhouse knew that fact but, for some reason, decided not to share it with me. They told my partner, Ed Dudley, but not me."

But Snead has yet to explain why he didn't try to find out for himself.

To jangle his nerves even more, he had to put up with a torturous delay before he could hit his drive. Fans, excited about seeing the next champion, began swarming onto the fairway. It took marshals nearly thirty minutes to clear the way from tee to green.

"I was stewing every second of it," he recalled. "I wanted to let off a shotgun blast to make those people jump out of my way. I thought about my folks, and about how hard I'd worked and practiced and prayed to get there, and how big a difference in my bank account a win could make.

"And as I'm pacing up and down there waiting for folks to simmer down and clear the green, not one of those folks saw fit to come over and say, 'Hold on there, Mr. Snead. Just relax and you'll breeze right into it.' Instead, I figured I had no more than four shots, which meant I'd have to birdie the hole if I wanted to avoid a play-off.

"When it finally came time to tee up, my teeth were nearly chattering from the tension."

He hit the ball too hard, hooking his drive into the rough, where it landed in a bare, sandy lie about 260 yards from the green. Conventional wisdom called for him to lay up and then pitch from that spot. But he was gunning for a birdie.

Although it's against the rules for one competitor to offer advice to another during play, Dudley, the head pro at the Philadelphia Country Club, apparently tried to give Sam a subtle hint by waving and swinging an iron from the rough on the opposite side of the fairway.

But Snead didn't take the hint. "Instead of trying to jump back on the fairway and proceeding from there, I took a chance," he recalled. "I decided that my best bet was to aim directly for the flag, and for that I used my trusty two wood. But I muffed that shot, connecting high on the ball."

The ball never got up, and it skidded into a bunker about 110 yards from the green in a partly buried lie about five feet down from the lip of the trap.

"I made a crazy attempt to perform a miracle," he said. "Deciding a sand iron wouldn't make my miracle, I used an eight, which gave the ball lots of power but not much loft."

His gamble didn't pay off. The ball slammed into the face of the bunker between two chunks of fresh-laid sod at the lip. The gallery let out a shocked groan and watched as the dumbstruck golfer slowly shook his head in anguish.

Snead then tried to explode the ball out, and it flew for about forty yards, only to find another bunker. Before Snead struck his fifth shot, a member of the gallery told him, "Nelson finished at 284. If you get out in two more, you'll tie him."

"Why didn't someone tell me that back on the tee so that I could have played it safe?" Snead snapped.

No one answered him.

Taking a few deep breaths to calm down, Snead drew out his nine iron and then squatted in an awkward stance with the ball below his feet. Choking up on the club, he practically scooped the ball onto the green to within forty feet of the pin.

Snead needed the putt to set up a possible play-off. "I had one last chance. Everything was now depending on my putt. I knew that if I made this last shot, I'd have a chance against Nelson in the play-off."

For a moment it looked like a miracle putt. The ball tracked toward the hole, followed the break, tickled the lip of the cup, and rolled past, leaving him with an irrelevant three-footer.

"Things got black then," he recalled. "I don't remember seeing a flash go off, but a picture of me appeared in the papers a few days later, and I looked like a man who'd lost his best friend.

"Not giving a damn anymore, I flubbed the three-footer, then finally sent that ball home for a total of eight strokes. When I leaned over to pull my ball out, that cup looked like the Black Hole of Calcutta. It has haunted me ever since."

Because of his triple bogey, Snead finished two strokes out of the play-off. Denny Shute and Craig Wood, who played behind Sam, tied Nelson at 284, forcing a three-man play-off, which Nelson won the next day.

Recalled Snead, "That night I was ready to go out with a gun and pay somebody to shoot me. It weighed on my mind so much that I dropped ten pounds, lost more hair, and began to choke up even on practice rounds."

Snead never did win an Open. He came close, finishing second in 1947, 1949, and 1953.

"If I'd won that thing like I should have in 1939," said Sam, "I think I'd have won seven or eight Opens."

Mike Reid
1989 PGA Championship

During the most memorable tournament of his life, Mike Reid knew exactly where he stood—in deep trouble.

He's known affectionately on the PGA Tour as "Radar" because he has been splitting fairways with uncanny accuracy ever since he turned pro in 1977. But his radar failed him at the most crucial time he could ever imagine—the final three holes of the 1989 PGA Championship.

Reid, who has never won a major, came close earlier in the year when he led the Masters with five holes left. But he bogeyed the fourteenth and double-bogeyed the fifteenth to finish sixth. "Call it a learning experience, a stepping-stone rather than a tombstone," he said at the time. "I don't view it as a defeat or a letdown. As Fuzzy Zoeller once said, 'I was happy to be in a position to choke.'"

Reid—who had won only two tournaments in his thirteen-year career at this point—came to the 7,197-yard Kemper Lakes Golf Course in suburban Chicago hoping for a decent showing at the PGA. He did better than that. He shot rounds of sixty-six, sixty-seven, and seventy for a thirteen-under 203, good for a three-stroke lead as he began the final round.

Reid made only his third bogey of the tourney when he three-putted the fifth hole. Now five players were within two shots of the lead. "I wasn't playing particularly well, but I felt in control of my game," Reid recalled. "When I needed a gut check, I got it, except for the bogey on number five. I thought if I ever got my rhythm, watch out."

Payne Stewart, resplendent in his plus fours that matched the colors of the hometown Chicago Bears, was four shots behind Reid at the turn. But Payne told ABC roving reporter Jerry Pate, "I can shoot thirty-one on the back nine and still win."

No one really believed him, especially when Radar birdied the tenth and eleventh holes to regain his three-stroke lead. But Stewart, playing three groups ahead, blistered the back nine with five birdies to pull within two of Reid.

Back on the sixteenth hole, Radar's accuracy began to waver. He pushed his tee shot into the water. "I was trying to cut my drive into the middle of the fairway and the Russians must have been transmitting," Reid said afterward. "My radar got zapped." But he managed to rescue a bogey five there by draining a curling, knee-knocking eight-footer. "When I made that putt for bogey, I thought I was okay," recalled Reid, who now had a one-shot lead with two holes left.

But on the par-three seventeenth, he sailed his four iron to the back fringe of the green, twenty-five feet above the hole just off the collar. Rather than chipping and running the ball to the hole, Reid tried a lob shot. But it came up fifteen feet short. "I couldn't putt the ball from the fringe because sometimes it will pop right up," he recalled, "so I tried to play it like a bunker shot. But I didn't follow through with it."

He needed to make this putt to save par. But the ball grazed the cup and stopped two feet away. "I thought I hit a good first putt, but it was too hard."

As he tried to regroup, Reid knew that once he sank his bogey putt, he still would be in a position to win the PGA on the final hole with a birdie. But the gallery gasped in horror when his second putt hit the right side of the cup and spun out. Reid had just made a double-bogey five and now trailed Stewart by a stroke. Radar needed a birdie on the final hole just to stay alive and force a play-off.

"There was a big crowd around the eighteenth tee, and they cheered for me," Reid recalled. "They wanted me to do it, to birdie the hole and tie the guy in the Bears outfit. I had never heard that before. I've always been so anonymous. But all four days these people were great to me."

His drive split the fairway, and he hit his approach to within seven feet of the hole. Reid was now faced with the biggest putt of his life. Purging his mind of the troubles he had on the sixteenth and seventeenth, he struck the ball firmly—and yanked it to the left. The plug had been pulled on Radar's dream of winning a major. The crushed golfer tapped in for par and a two-over seventy-four for the round. He tied Andy Bean and Curtis Strange for second with an eleven-under 277.

When Reid missed his putt, Stewart, who had been pacing nervously in the scorer's tent, dashed outside and began high-fiving friends and fellow golfers, including a disheartened Reid. In the clubhouse later, Jack Nicklaus put an arm around Reid and told him, "I just want to say that I've never felt so bad for anyone in my life. You played too well not to win."

An hour after the awards ceremony, Reid—his face drawn and his eyes red—visited the press tent. "Oh, boy," he mumbled into the microphone. "Where can you go around here to have a good cry?"

The press tent seemed as good a place as any. So right there, in front of TV cameras and hardened reporters, Mike Reid broke down and shamelessly wept. No one knew what to say or do, so everyone sat silently and watched the veteran golfer sob over blowing the PGA Championship.

Finally, Reid composed himself and told the crowd, "It's okay. I cry at supermarket openings." His self-effacing crack broke the tension and brought a big laugh.

But it was still hard for him to talk about the pain he was feeling. "I led through fourteen at the Masters and through sixteen here. I'm getting there. One of these days I'll finish it and get it right." Fighting back more tears, he croaked, "This hurts."

After taking a few deep breaths, he added, "I'm happy for Payne, but sad for me. It's only a game, right? Everybody can identify with failure out here. You can't play textbook golf. Sports is like life with the volume turned up. The friendships are tighter, the laughter is louder, and some nights seem a little longer, like tonight is going to be when I'm trying to figure out what happened. I'll go back to the hotel and cry. Yeah, I'll cry big-time."

Reid had hoped to build on the painful experiences of 1989 when he came oh-so-close to winning two majors. But it didn't work out that way for him. He never won another PGA Tour event (through 1997) and never finished in the top twenty-five of another major.

"At the time you think, because you're playing well, you're going to have other opportunities," Reid said recently. "I guess the thing I regret the most is you just don't realize at the time how few chances you have. You don't think you're going to disappear from view like I have.

"Those opportunities don't come along very often. As much as you try to imagine and prepare for them, it's like being on a tightrope without a net. I wasn't thinking too clearly on a couple of mistakes I made."

He tries not to dwell on the missed opportunities. "You can let it bother you if you want to, or you can realize there aren't many guys who ever get in that situation, and you must have been doing something well. You try to build on it instead of just let it consume you."

THE ATLANTA NIGHTMARE

Patty Sheehan
1990 U.S. Women's Open

Patty Sheehan arrived at the 1990 U.S. Women's Open with her mind full of positive, upbeat thoughts. She left with a head full of golf demons that haunted her for the next two years.

That's how long it took for her to get over one of the LPGA's worst single-day collapses in a women's major. Unlike most downfalls, hers was caused more by physical exhaustion rather than mental meltdown.

The tournament at the Atlanta Athletic Club began on such a positive note for Patty. Firing a six-under sixty-six in the first round to join Jane Geddes at the top of the leader board, Sheehan was one of nineteen players who shot subpar rounds on the Riverside Course. It seemed so easy that many of the golfers boldly criticized the course for being "unexciting," "not intimidating," and "not challenging."

Patty was moved to admit at the time, "I like an Open course to be tough. It sorts the good players out from the okay players. That's what you want."

Unfortunately for her, Sheehan fell victim to that old adage: Be careful what you ask for; you just might get it. In her case, she got more than she bargained for.

Part of her misfortune could be blamed on the streak of old-fashioned bad luck that had cursed the Women's Open. In 1986 at the NCR Country Club in Dayton, Ohio, the tournament experienced one mishap after another: A train crash sent foul smoke across the countryside; a rare earthquake shook the area; a tornado touched down nearby; a private plane crash-landed in an adjacent field, knocking down a fence, which let cattle graze on the tournament site. The following year, rain washed out Sunday's final round and the Open wasn't concluded until Tuesday. Rain struck again at the 1988 event but wasn't a factor the next year.

In 1990, however, rain caused havoc at the Atlanta Athletic Club—two rain delays on Thursday, three on Friday, and a six-hour delay at the

A weary and dehydrated Patty Sheehan sags as her birdie putt on the eighteenth hole fails to drop.

start on Saturday. More than four inches of rain fell in the first three days, surpassing the area's rainfall for the previous three months.

As coleader, Patty was itching to complete the second round. Like many golfers, she was starting to get her rhythm when officials ordered everyone off the course because of the rain. Play resumed, only to be interrupted again. Finally, it got too dark and wet for nearly half the players to finish their round.

The plan called for a resumption of play at 7 A.M. Saturday for those golfers who hadn't completed their second round, but a morning deluge saturated Riverside and delayed play until 1 P.M. As a result, the only golfers who played on Saturday were those who needed to complete the second round.

Despite the annoying rain delays on Friday and Saturday, Patty shot sixty-eight, the round's only subseventy score. Her ten-under 134 at the halfway mark gave her a commanding six-stroke lead over Geddes, her closest competitor, and nine strokes over defending champion Betsy King.

There was a downside for Patty. Many golfers who had finished their second round on Friday rested on Saturday, while she had to stay late on the course to complete her round. Then she received the unwanted news that all golfers would have to play thirty-six holes on Sunday, an unprecedented grind never before attempted at a U.S. Women's Open. It was a decision that triggered a volley of heavy criticism—and led to disaster for Patty.

Sheehan had to report at the crack of dawn the next day. Frazzled and drained by the strange week, Patty ate little for breakfast before embarking on the most painful day of her life.

The rains gave way to the hot, steamy summer weather that Atlanta is known for. Although she wasn't feeling physically strong, the thirty-three-year-old golfer surprised herself by making birdies on the second and third holes in the morning round to go twelve under for the tournament. That score was three strokes better than anyone else had ever reached at any time in a Women's Open. She pushed her lead to a whopping nine strokes with twenty-seven holes to play.

But then Patty hit the wall.

"I had no fuel onboard when I went out, which was a huge mistake," she later recalled. "I started losing it. I was dehydrated. My body couldn't work. I couldn't think properly, and I had no strength."

Every shot in the third round became an effort for Sheehan, who felt grateful whenever she made par because she seldom had a chance at another birdie. As her body began to betray her, she bogeyed three times over the next fourteen holes.

When she reached the 523-yard, par-five eighteenth, Patty still had a six-stroke lead over Mary Murphy. But then Sheehan drove into the right rough and hit her recovery heavy, leaving her a four iron requiring a 150-yard carry over water to the green. She hit her third shot fat and watched it dive into the drink guarding the left front of the green. She dropped, hit the green, and two-putted for a double-bogey seven, finishing her third round in a three-over seventy-five.

Sheehan's total of 209 was now only four strokes ahead of Murphy and five ahead of King, who earlier in the day had trailed by as many as eleven strokes.

Weary and dismayed, Patty had a mere thirty-five minutes to gulp down some lunch before she headed out for the final round. Throughout the front nine, Sheehan looked wobbly and uncertain. "I felt like I was going to pass out during those first seven holes," she recalled.

Patty didn't faint, but she did fade. She bogeyed the par-four second hole, par-three sixth, and par-three eighth, while King birdied the par-five third and par-four fourth. On the ninth tee, the two were dead even—and Patty was dead tired.

She bogeyed the ninth, playing the front nine in a dismal forty, and made the turn with King, who, having parred the hole earlier, was now in the lead. Betsy increased the margin with a birdie on the par-three eleventh.

But Patty still had some fire left in her. Despite her unsteady legs, she mustered birdies on the par-four fourteenth and par-four fifteenth holes to tie King.

After parring the sixteenth, Patty needed to par the final two holes to set up a play-off with King. Minutes earlier, Betsy finished with a two-under seventy and a four-under 284 for the tournament. King, who had beaten Patty in a play-off in the 1987 Nabisco Dinah Shore, waited in the clubhouse.

But by now Sheehan's body was running only on fumes. On the 180-yard, par-three seventeenth, she sent her tee shot into the right front bunker. Then she launched her ball twenty-five feet past the hole and missed her par putt.

Simply to survive, Patty needed to birdie the par-five eighteenth, the same hole she had double-bogeyed earlier in the day. She sent her drive and second shot straight down the fairway, and was now near the same spot where she had rinsed her ball in the third round. Fighting back the wooziness, Sheehan lofted her approach onto the green, but about twenty feet from the hole.

Once again she faced a crucial long putt. Trying to ignore the debilitating mental and physical fatigue, she lined up her putt—and missed. Patty slumped her shoulders and then halfheartedly tapped in for par.

Sheehan—the LPGA's leading money winner at the time—had shot seventy-six, ten strokes higher than her opening-round score. Her total of 285 was one stroke behind King, who claimed her second straight Women's Open championship.

Suffering from what was quickly diagnosed as dehydration and hypoglycemia, Patty staggered into the locker room. There she spent the next hour sobbing with friends and wondering why her body had let her down at such a crucial time.

"If I had played like this the first two rounds," Patty said after emerging from the locker room, "I'd have missed the cut [by two strokes]. I just didn't feel well all day. I tried to overcome it, but I couldn't. It's not the end of the world. I tried very, very hard. It just wasn't my week. I played superbly for two rounds, and then it just wasn't there."

Betsy sympathized with her teary-eyed opponent, telling reporters, "Obviously, I felt like I won the event more last year [winning by four strokes]. But that happens. Lots of times you win events and you don't play that well. They're not going to know that happened down the road. They're just going to see the winner's name and not know what occurred."

But Patty Sheehan will always know.

"I believe in turning negatives into positives," Patty said years later. "But Atlanta was so disappointing, so devastating, that it just kept grinding on me."

She confessed the Atlanta nightmare haunted her "every day" for the next two years. The golf demons kept replaying those horrible moments in her mind.

Not until the 1992 U.S. Women's Open in Oakmont did she finally exorcise those demons. She had decided before the tournament that "the Open shouldn't become so important that it disrupts my inner harmony as it had in the past."

Stocking up on rest and fluids to prevent a repeat of her physical collapse in Atlanta, a relaxed Sheehan made a late charge. She knocked in a clutch fifteen-foot birdie putt to force an eighteen-hole play-off with Juli Inkster, which Patty won the next day. Two months later she captured the British Women's Open—the first golfer to garner both titles in the same year.

Those victories, another U.S. Women's Open win in 1994, and her induction into the LPGA Hall of Fame that same year proved to be the talismans she needed to keep the demons away for good.

The nightmare at the 1990 Open "doesn't hurt anymore," Patty said recently. "I don't feel anger as to why things happened the way they did. All that resentment for decisions that were made that week [by tournament officials] is gone now, too. Thank God I was able to win an Open and get rid of all the demons. Had I not won, I'm sure the disappointment would be with me the rest of my life."

John Mahaffey
1976 U.S. Open

Under circumstances similar to those of Patty Sheehan, John Mahaffey fell victim to calamity at the very same Atlanta Athletic Club during the rain-plagued 1976 U.S. Open.

Mahaffey had built a hefty lead—six strokes with twenty-seven holes to play on the ACC's Highlands Course. But then a vicious lightning storm struck, halting play for nearly two hours. The delay threw off his rhythm, and he finished the back nine in near darkness. By day's end, his lead had shrunk to only two strokes.

"I lost my concentration," John admitted. "It was a long day."

The twenty-eight-year-old golfer desperately wanted to win because he had come so close the year before. In the 1975 Open, he let a lead slip away and lost in a thrilling eighteen-hole play-off against Lou Graham at Medinah Country Club.

Mahaffey was seeking redemption at the 1976 Open. Following the dark, wet third round, Mahaffey said, "After losing last year, I'm more determined than ever to win this tournament. We'll find out how mentally tough I am tomorrow."

He already knew that his physical strength was waning. "I drove short today—don't know what's wrong," he admitted to the press. "I'm not very happy with my length off the tee. I had to go to too many greens with woods. I'm dead tired—but anxious to play tomorrow."

In the final round, Mahaffey couldn't power the ball far enough. He simply ran out of steam. Even though his swing was fine and he deftly handled the perilous fairways, he gave away precious yards on each hole to longer hitters like rookie Jerry Pate and veterans Tom Weiskopf and Al Geiberger.

Mahaffey still led by one stroke with three holes to play, but he lost his concentration and, after bogeying the sixteenth and seventeenth, the lead.

Then came his moment of truth. Faced with a difficult lie in the right rough of the last hole, Mahaffey attempted a three wood to the green for a chance at a birdie to tie Pate, the new leader. But the power was gone. Mahaffey sent his ball into the water in front of the green and bogeyed his third straight hole.

Shooting a three-over seventy-three for the day, the dejected golfer finished in a fourth-place tie at an even-par 280 with Butch Baird, a forty-year-old fringe Tour player.

"Certainly the dumbest shot I ever hit was when I tried to go for the green on my second shot at the eighteenth," Mahaffey admitted years later. "I hit some pretty good shots those last three holes, but still ended up with three bogeys. I just looked at the Open as a great test of golf. I'd like to be in that position again."

His tribulations continued off the course in 1976 and 1977. He went through a divorce, hyperextended his elbow, and battled a thumb injury. Just when he was ready to get back on track, he suffered a broken wrist from a fall off a ladder in his workshop. The setbacks dropped him from eighth on the money list to 149th in 1977, when he earned a paltry $9,847. There were doubts among his fellow golfers that he would ever win again.

"It was excruciating, very traumatic, for a while," Mahaffey admitted. "It wasn't my personal problems, nor my injuries, nor either Open that affected me. It was a combination of all of them."

But his woes vanished when he charged from seven strokes back to win the 1978 PGA Championship at Oakmont (the same site that Patty Sheehan won her first U.S. Open). Firing rounds of seventy-five, sixty-seven, sixty-eight, and sixty-six, Mahaffey caught leaders Jerry Pate and Tom Watson, forcing a sudden-death play-off. Mahaffey then drilled a birdie putt on the second extra hole for an emotionally draining victory.

Ironically, he won his first and only major because of gaffes made by his competitors. Pate—the man who beat him in the 1976 U.S. Open—three-putted the final hole. Watson, who led the field by four strokes at the turn, bogeyed three of the four par threes and double-bogeyed the tenth. (Watson didn't let the defeat shake his confidence. He won five major titles over the next five years. But he has yet to win the PGA—the one championship keeping him from a career Grand Slam.)

"At the '78 PGA," Mahaffey said, "I finally realized the thing people had told me in the past: You can't make yourself win; you've got to let yourself win. And that's what happened that day. I let myself win."

He said the championship revamped his life. "I learned you just have to be persistent."

Black Holes

Tiger Woods finds himself deep in yet another bunker in the final round of the British Open after suffering two earlier misadventures in Troon's gorse.

UNNATURAL DISASTERS

Tiger Woods
1997 British Open

Tiger Woods was one of the favorites to win the 1997 British Open. But he never got close enough to battle for the silver Claret Jug. He was ambushed by three misadventures at Scotland's Royal Troon Golf Club.

In the opening round, Tiger zigged and zagged his way through hummocks, potholes, and gorse—the low, prickly evergreen shrub that gobbles up golf balls. Besides his playing partners, the twenty-one-year-old phenom was accompanied by four Royal Marine commandos wearing bright-blue jackets and carrying umbrellas, even though the sun was shining brightly. The bodyguards—unprecedented in 126 years of the British Open—kept the fans at bay but couldn't protect him from Royal Troon's wicked pitfalls.

Woods played the downwind front nine in one-under thirty-five. Then he turned into a steady breeze blowing off the Firth of Clyde. After parring the tenth, he suffered his first calamity of the tournament on the 463-yard, par-four eleventh, which is nicknamed "The Railway" because it's bordered on the right by the Glasgow-Ayr railway tracks.

Tiger was preparing to hit his tee shot when a train roared past. The engineer tooted the horn and waved. "I stepped back because I could see him coming before I entered the shot," Tiger told the press later. "It wasn't a distraction. Then I made a bad swing."

Woods's drive landed in thick gorse on the right side. He took a penalty drop because of an unplayable lie. Then he tried to force a two iron, but it caught a hill and stopped in the thick rough 120 yards short of the green. His eight iron sailed over the green and stopped on the back fringe. After chipping to within six feet, he missed his putt and tapped in for a triple-bogey seven.

(If it was any consolation, Jack Nicklaus took a ten on this hole in his first British Open at Troon in 1962 when he was twenty-two years old.)

Tiger recovered nicely and, with the help of birdies on the sixteenth and eighteenth, finished the day at one-over seventy-two, five shots off the pace.

Despite his misfortune on the eleventh, he was pleased he never lost his patience. "You would have probably thought I would have, but I never lost it," he told reporters.

"When you play in wind like this, it's going to be hard work because you're going to make some bad swings. You have to scramble and hang in there. Rounds under these conditions are going to test your patience."

He rated the eleventh as the toughest hole on the 7,079-yard seaside course. But the worst was yet to come.

Unlike the windblown first round, conditions on Friday were nearly perfect—hardly the time or place to think about a snowman. But that's what appeared on his scorecard after he tangled with the flora on the 438-yard, par-four tenth.

Tiger, who played the front nine in even par, hit his three wood off the tee and knocked the ball into the left rough. He caught a flier with his eight iron approach and watched it go over the green and into the rough in front of a gorse bush.

Woods tried to play a shot to the front of the green, but he whiffed a sand wedge, missing the ball entirely when his club caught the bush behind him. Then he hacked the ball out about eighteen feet. His chip was just short of the green, so he chipped again, this time to within twelve feet of the cup. Finally, he two-putted for a quadruple-bogey eight.

He finished the round at three-over seventy-four. His two-round total of four-over 146 made the cut by two shots and left him a distant thirteen strokes behind the leader.

"It's just one of those things where I had a high number at the wrong time," he said of his troubles on the tenth. Then, in an understatement, he added, "It was not a good hole."

Eight was more than enough for Tiger, who had impressed the gray and gnarled members of Troon with his poise following the two bad holes.

All but promising to shoot a low number in the third round, Woods backed up his words. He tied Greg Norman's course record with a seven-under sixty-four, which included an eagle on the par-five sixteenth. That round put him three under for fifty-four holes, but still eight shots back of new leader Jesper Parnevik.

Had Woods been able to par the eleventh in the first round and the tenth in the second round, he would have been only one stroke behind Parnevik.

Tiger was hoping to duplicate his third-round score on the final day. But he spent much of the time ankle deep in grass—and more time than he ever wanted to spend at the eighth hole, the 126-yard par three known as the "Postage Stamp."

Even though it's the shortest hole on the course, it has confounded golfers for decades. The hole plays from an elevated tee to a tiny, narrow green surrounded by five bunkers that swallow balls the way black holes absorb light. In 1950, Hermann Tissies, Germany's renowned golfer at the time, recorded the highest single-hole score in modern British Open history at the eighth—a bungling fifteen.

Tiger didn't come close to that "horrible species of Ping-Pong played between the bunkers" as the local newspaper described Tissies's tragicomedy. But Woods still took a licking at the Postage Stamp.

When he reached the eighth, he was two under for the round and looking more at a strong finish than a challenge for the championship. But then he drove his nine iron into the far right bunker, where his ball was buried. He tried to blast out, but the ball rolled right back in.

After taking a couple of deep breaths, he tried to blast out again. This time he was successful, sort of. His ball flew out of the bunker, but landed way too long. From there, he took three putts for a triple-bogey six. (FYI: Gene Sarazen aced this hole in the 1973 British Open—at the age of seventy-one.)

Tiger finished at three-over seventy-four for the round and an even-par 284, good for a twenty-fourth-place tie. He was twelve shots behind winner Justin Leonard. Had Woods parred those three blowup holes, he would have finished no worse than second and could arguably have made a successful run for the title.

"The week wasn't bad, but I had three bad holes," said Woods. "You can't afford to let that happen in a major. Overall, it was a good experience."

Said his swing doctor, Butch Harmon, "All of this is a learning process for him. He's never played a golf course like Troon that's so demanding and testing of your patience. As long as you learn something from it and use it to your advantage it's all right."

Mark Brooks
1991 Las Vegas Invitational

At least the members of the gallery didn't laugh at Tiger Woods's misfortune the way they did at Mark Brooks's woes during the 1991 Las Vegas Invitational.

If Mark had the same luck at the gaming tables that he had on the course, he would have walked out of the casino in his shorts.

He can laugh about it now, but he doesn't like to talk about it—at least not for this book, for which he declined to be interviewed. Tournament director Charlie Baron, however, provided the details of Brooks's most embarrassing tourney.

"I don't think I'd be exaggerating to say there's never been anything like it in the history of professional golf," claimed Baron. "What that guy went through is just amazing."

Brooks, winner that year of the Kmart Greater Greensboro Open and Greater Milwaukee Open, had shot rounds of sixty-seven and sixty-five at the five-day multicourse tournament in Las Vegas. As luck would have it, this was the event in which Chip Beck fired a PGA record-tying fifty-nine.

Nevertheless, Brooks was in the thick of the chase when his errant drive on the seventeenth hole lodged about thirty feet up in a palm tree on the Desert Inn course. "Mark needed to find his ball, so we got him a big extension ladder and he climbed up to the top with some binoculars," recalled Baron.

Brooks poked around through the fronds and gathered eight balls. But, to his disappointment, none were his. After his futile search, he took his driver, walked back to the tee, and hit again with loss of stroke and distance. "By then he was kind of frazzled because he had lost his ball, backed up play, and knew his chance to catch the leader was fading," said Baron. Mark, who double-bogeyed the hole, shot seventy-four for the round.

The next day, his mishaps continued. And it had nothing to do with his swing. It had all to do with his throw.

At the Las Vegas Country Club, Brooks played the back nine first. On his last hole, the par-three ninth, he sent his tee shot onto the green and was putting for birdie. He marked his ball, picked it up, and tossed it to his caddie. But his caddie wasn't looking. The ball sailed past his face and right into a greenside lake.

The rules say a player will be penalized two strokes if he doesn't complete the hole with the same ball that he played off the tee. So Brooks took off his shoes and socks, rolled up his pants, and waded into the water. He fished around with his hands and feet, pulling up ball after ball.

"That lake is pretty deep there, and before it was over Mark was in up to his shoulders and covered with gunk," Baron recalled. "He'd see a ball and reach down to get it and throw it up onto the bank and find that it wasn't his. But every time he reached down he stirred up the muck on the bottom and it got harder to see the balls."

Brooks found eighteen balls. Alas, not one of them was his.

"The whole time the crowd was just roaring with laughter," said Baron. "He was in there splashing around. You couldn't help but laugh because it was just so comical. After about five minutes, Mark gave up and he came out of the lake looking like the Swamp Thing. It was unbelievable. Everyone, including Mark, was laughing."

Soaking wet, Brooks tromped back to the tee and hit again. Because of the penalty, he ended up with a double-bogey five and a seventy-eight for the round.

In the tournament, Brooks found a total of twenty-six lost balls, all belonging to other unlucky golfers—but none as unlucky as he was.

"Not many people know what happened the next day," said Baron. "Mark was set to go off first. Because we had an odd number in the field, he had an option to play with a 'marker' player to help his timing. He said, 'Charlie, I'll play a single. Just do me one favor—make sure the lady scorer has her sneakers on today because we're going to try and set a new course record.'

"Well, he wasn't talking about scoring. After he teed off, he and his caddie broke into a trot and they ran through that round. The scorer told me later that it was very invigorating. Mark shot seventy-five that day. He ended up dead last and earned $2,850. He finished that round in an unofficial record of one hour and forty-five minutes. And then, zoom, he was gone. It was like he wanted to get away as soon as he could.

"Mark still laughs about Las Vegas whenever he sees me. He doesn't say much. He just shakes his head like he can't believe it really happened."

THE UNFORGETTABLE

Arnold Palmer
1961 Los Angeles Open
1964 Bing Crosby National Pro-Am

Arnold Palmer says he tries to put bad holes out of his mind. "We're all going to have bad holes. You just have to forget about it."

But how do you forget about it when your worst hole ever has been commemorated with a bronze plaque? Such a marker sits on the ninth tee at the Rancho Park Golf Course for all to snicker over.

"Yeah, that's one I'll never forget," Arnie recalled with a grin. "How can I? That plaque is still there."

In the first round of the 1961 Los Angeles Open, the General shot an atrocious twelve on the ninth hole—after blasting four straight balls out of bounds.

As the defending U.S. Open and Masters champion, Palmer was on the heels of the leaders coming to the 508-yard, par-five ninth, his finishing hole. A par would give him a sixty-nine. But Arnie was gunning for a birdie, which would put him only two shots behind the pace setters.

After hitting a good drive, Palmer decided against laying up at a spot where the fairway narrowed to a bottleneck in front of the green. "I wanted the green in two," Palmer recalled. "I knew that laying up with irons would keep me from going OB right and left. It was tight, so I pulled out a three wood for better control."

Unfortunately, Arnie didn't have the control he had hoped for. "At first I thought I had hit a good shot," he said. "But the ball began drifting to the right." He expected it to land just inside the thirty-foot-high chain-link fence that separated the driving range from the fairway. "I figured I would get a free drop and still have a chance for birdie. But it came down right on top of a galvanized pipe on the fence and kicked right, into the driving range."

That cost him one penalty stroke, so he dropped another ball and aimed for the green once again. "On my second shot from the fairway I overcorrected the problem. I hooked it clear out of the course on the opposite side of the fairway and clear out on the road. A little steam came off my head then."

As tournament officials—and a stray dog—look on, Arnold Palmer flails away on the rocks, trying to get his ball back to civilization at Pebble Beach.

Another penalty stroke, another dropped ball. Still sticking with his three wood, Arnie blasted away. "I pushed that one in almost the same spot as the first one, and it went over the [practice range] fence, too."

Palmer was no longer concerned about his runaway score. This had turned into a personal battle: Palmer versus the ninth hole. After another drop and penalty stroke, he swung his three wood for the fourth time. It was an exact repeat of his previous hook into traffic.

Now lying nine, Arnie remained with his three wood. "I will always go for it and believe I'm going to make it," he said. "That time I was wrong. I was wrong a bunch of times that day. I just kept coming up short." It took him five attempts with that three wood before he hit it straight and onto the green. From there, Palmer two-putted for his inglorious twelve—the most horrendous score he had ever recorded for one hole in a tournament.

"In one hole, I went from among the leaders in the tournament to missing the cut. The reporters asked me later, 'Arnie, how could you make a twelve on one hole?' I said, 'It was simple. I missed a twenty-foot putt for an eleven. It's a nice round figure, that twelve. This should give the duffers a bit of heart.'"

Actually, it has. In honor of his infamous score, a bronze plaque on a stone pedestal was installed at the ninth hole to remind all weekend hackers that at times they, too, can be just as "good" as Arnold Palmer. The plaque reads: "On Friday, Jan. 6, 1961, the first day of the 35th Los Angeles Open, Arnold Palmer, voted Golfer of the Year and Pro Athlete of the Year, took a 12 on this hole."

Palmer flashes his trademark smile whenever he thinks about that marker. "That doggone plaque will be there long after I'm gone. But you have to put things like that behind you. That's one of the wonderful things about golf. Your next shot can be as good or as bad as your last one—but you'll always get another chance."

In hindsight, Arnie was asked, should he have hit an iron on his second shot and laid up? "No," Palmer replied. "I'd still go for it."

At least Palmer's twelve wasn't seen on television. One of his most embarrassing moments on the course, however, *was* witnessed by millions of TV viewers. History refers to it as the "Palmer on the Rocks" incident. It happened on the seventeenth hole at Pebble Beach during the third round of the 1964 Bing Crosby National Pro-Am.

The 218-yard par-three ran toward the sea to a green flanked by rocks and the Pacific Ocean. Arnie hit his tee shot over the cliff behind the green, into shallow water in front of the eighteenth tee. The bay and its beaches were then played as part of the course. They were not lateral water hazards, which would have allowed a golfer to drop the ball on dry land with a penalty stroke. (The local rule was later abolished, and the beaches are now considered water hazards.)

As a national TV audience watched in amazement, Palmer stood there, with a curious stray dog behind him, and pondered his shot. Roving TV reporter Jimmy Demaret told viewers the options under the unplayable ball rule: "If he takes the option of dropping behind the point where the ball rests, keeping in line with the pin, his nearest drop is Honolulu."

Palmer gamely flailed away on the rocky beach as his ball bounded from one large stone to another. It took him six shots to get the ball off the beach and onto the green in the seventeen-minute televised drama. Arnie then two-putted for a lamentable nine.

Jim Murray, famed columnist of the *Los Angeles Times*, described the scene from the vantage point of his living-room TV set: "Palmer . . . was so far out on a moor in the ocean he looked like Robinson Crusoe. His only companions were a dog and a sand wedge. I thought for a minute we had switched channels and Walt Disney was bringing us another of those heart-warming stories of a boy and his dog. But a companion, peering closely, had a better idea: 'Shouldn't that dog have a cask around his neck?'"

That same nasty hole vexed Palmer a year earlier when his two iron shot flew over the green and disappeared, apparently lost in the water. Invoking the lost-ball rule, Arnie hit another shot from the tee. But when his first ball was found lying on the rocks on the beach, he played that onto the green.

The next day, PGA officials ruled that Palmer had struck an unauthorized provisional ball; that he, in effect, had abandoned his first ball the moment he hit the second one. He was disqualified, even though he had finished the final round. As a result of his DQ, Palmer's string of forty-seven consecutive tournament finishes in the money was over.

Ray Ainsley
1938 U.S. Open

While Arnold Palmer's disaster is commemorated in bronze, Ray Ainsley's is etched in the record book.

Few people have ever heard of Ainsley, yet he made golfing history, achieving a mark that has never been matched by any pro in a major. Ainsley shot an amazing nineteen—for one hole!

Ray carded an incredible triple-triple-triple-triple-triple-bogey on the par-four sixteenth hole at Cherry Hills Country Club in Denver during the second round of the 1938 U.S. Open.

The young Californian, playing in his first Open, had been shooting respectable golf, although he was never in contention. He would have been just another forgotten name in a long list of qualifiers if he hadn't swung his way to infamy on one hole.

After hooking his drive into the rough, he sent his second shot into a shallow, but swift-moving stream running in front of the green. His ball was plugged on a sandbar—but a few inches under the clear, cold water. Rather than take a drop, Ray figured he had a playable lie. Playable for a trout, maybe, but not a golfer.

Nevertheless, Ainsley took off his shoes and socks, drew a sand wedge out of his bag, and planted his feet in the creek. Just as he went into his swing, the current moved the ball downstream a few inches. Ray couldn't stop his swing and hit nothing but water and sand.

So he took a new stance and swung again . . . and again . . . and again. He missed each time because the current kept pushing the ball away from him a split second before his club would have hit it. Whacking away at the water with his iron, Ainsley was soaked and splattered with wet sand. But he refused to give up.

On the bank, Ray's playing partner, Bud McKinney, had jammed his fist into his mouth to keep from laughing. But official scorer Red Anderson, who was calling the strokes out loud, couldn't contain himself after the count reached nine. Falling on the ground in stitches, Anderson told McKinney between guffaws, "Take over the count, Bud."

So McKinney dutifully shouted, "Ten! . . . Eleven! . . . Twelve! . . ."

Finally, on the thirteenth stroke, Ainsley hit the ball. It soared out of the water like a Polaris missile—a misguided one. The ball crashed into a clump of bushes well beyond the green. The never-say-die Ray worked his way through the brush and found his ball. It took him three more strokes before the ball plopped onto the green. Then, as if a sixth sense told him that he could break the old record of eighteen, Ainsley three-putted. The record was his—the worst score ever for one hole in a pro championship.

"And everybody loved him for it," wrote Chester Nelson, sports editor of *The Rocky Mountain News,* who was covering the tournament. Nelson said Ray's dubious achievement was applauded by "all dubs [boneheads] who ever forgot to touch second base, all the dubs who ever ran backwards in the last quarter, and all the other dubs."

Recalling the time he dumped five straight balls into the drink on Augusta's twelfth hole, Tom Weiskopf admits, "If that had happened earlier in my career, I'd probably have jumped into the water."

DUNK SHOTS

Tom Weiskopf
1980 Masters

The twelfth hole in the heart of Amen Corner at Augusta National has been called many spiteful names. Gary Player pegged it the "Hole of Vultures," Fuzzy Zoeller said it's "the spookiest par three in golf," and 1940 Masters runner-up Lloyd Mangrum claimed it's "the meanest little hole in the world." Jack Nicklaus flatly declared the twelfth "the hardest tournament hole in golf."

Its official nickname is the "Golden Bell." It has rung the death knell for the hopes of many golfers. And the bell tolled most loudly for Tom Weiskopf.

He holds the record for the most strokes over par—a whopping ten —for a single hole in Masters history. He did it by plunking five straight balls into the drink at the twelfth for a horrendous thirteen.

In the opening round of the 1980 Masters, Weiskopf was struggling at three over when he reached the bucolic 155-yard par three. He was well aware of its reputation for looking like heaven but playing like hell. First off, the intimidating Rae's Creek fronts a green that has very little depth. Even worse are the tricky winds. The thirteenth fairway funnels the breezes directly to the twelfth green so that conditions at the tee are not necessarily those at the green. The flag on the green could be flapping in the breeze while the air at the tee is still. Seconds later, the wind could be blowing in the golfer's face at the tee while the flag is limp.

Although Weiskopf had a healthy respect for the hole, he didn't fear it. As a four-time Masters runner-up (1969, 1972, 1974, and 1975), he had parred this hole many times. Nevertheless, he knew he was subject to the vagaries of the wind. On this day, he seemed subject to the vagaries of the golf gods—and they were angry.

Weiskopf, one of the year's top money winners, pulled out his seven iron, confident that he could get the ball onto the green. His tee shot cleared the creek, but not by enough. As the gallery groaned, the ball trickled maddeningly back down the slope and into the water.

His playing partner, Tom Purtzer, hit safely onto the green. Walking down to the drop area partway between the tee and creek, Weiskopf received a new ball from his caddie. The drop area was still soggy from a heavy rain two days earlier, and the grass was extremely thin. From that spot, he hit a sand wedge and watched the ball clear the creek, only to spin back into the water just as the first shot had done.

Weiskopf, known for his flawless swing, stood ramrod straight for several seconds and, then, with a stone face, extended his right arm. His caddie silently put another ball into the golfer's outstretched hand. Once again, Weiskopf dropped, and once again he swung for the green, and once again his ball plopped into the creek. Staring straight ahead, Weiskopf stuck out his hand toward his caddie, never looking at him, and waited for another ball. Then Tom dropped it over his shoulder and knocked it into the water.

He found himself locked in a nightmarish, diabolical groove: hit . . . splash . . . drop . . . hit . . . splash . . . drop.

After soaking five straight balls, Weiskopf—still valiantly hiding any emotion—had used up ten strokes (including the penalty strokes). Finally, mercifully, on his sixth attempt (his eleventh shot), the ball landed on the back fringe of the green. He two-putted from there for a record-setting thirteen.

Tom's demeanor was as surprising as his score. Throughout this debacle, not once did Weiskopf—who had a reputation for throwing temper tantrums—flinch or mutter a word. When he finished the hole, however, he walked over to the bench at the thirteenth tee, sat down, and stared at the ground for a long time.

Maybe he should have let out a primal scream. He was still so rattled by his adversity that on the 475-yard, par-five hole, he tried for the green in two. "At that point I wasn't about to lay up," he recalled. "It became a challenge." Unfortunately, his three wood landed in Rae's Creek. He took a bogey six on the hole and finished the day with a mortifying eighty-five.

Weekend duffers can identify with someone who shoots a thirteen much more easily than they can with someone who makes an eagle. That's why when Weiskopf walked off the eighteenth green that day, the crowd showered him with a warm applause that he had never experienced before.

To his credit, Weiskopf fielded questions afterward in a calm manner. "If you think I'm composed, you're badly mistaken," he told reporters. "A lot of things went through my mind. I was afraid to move my lips in front of the TV cameras. The commissioner probably would have fined me for what I was thinking."

Acknowledging the crowd's reaction to him, he shook his head and said, "It was sympathy applause. It was extremely embarrassing. The last time I got a thirteen probably was when I was about fourteen years old.

I've never been so disappointed in my life. But I'll be there to tee off tomorrow."

When he approached the twelfth tee the following day, the gallery wondered how he would handle the hole. Would he act timid? Would he attack it? Could he forget about the dunkings of yesterday, or would the fresh memories bedevil him?

The crowd grew so silent it seemed all the spectators were holding their breath at the same time. Seconds later, they let out a collective moan as Weiskopf, incredibly, plunked his tee shot into the water. But this time, he didn't take a drop. Instead, he switched clubs, teed off again—and plopped another into the creek.

The Masters was over for him, and he knew it. "But I just wasn't going to give up," he recalled. "I mean, that was a challenge."

Not wanting to bear witness to Weiskopf's growing embarrassment, some people in the gallery turned away as the grim-faced golfer prepared to fire again. This time, he reached the green and finished the hole with a sorry quadruple-bogey seven. On the bright side, it was quite an improvement from the day before. On the other hand, the Masters veteran had played the twelfth in fourteen over par on consecutive days.

He shot seventy-nine in the second round to go with his deplorable first-round eighty-five. (Weiskopf's 164, combined with the 174 of playing partner Doug Clarke, an amateur, probably set a Masters record for thirty-six-hole futility by a twosome.)

When reporters asked fellow golfer Tom Watson for his reaction to Weiskopf's water troubles, Watson shuddered and said, "I'm not saying anything because it could happen to me." It did the very next day. He splashed two into Rae's Creek on the twelfth.

Years later, Weiskopf reflected on his inglorious disaster. "The thing was, I was trying to get over the water but couldn't. It got so absurd it was funny. I had to laugh at myself. But if that had happened earlier in my career, I'd probably have jumped into the water, too.

"After it happened, I got a lot of sympathetic letters. A few fans even sent me floating golf balls."

Tommy Nakajima
1978 Masters

Tom Weiskopf shares the record for the highest score on a hole in Masters history with Tommy Nakajima, who, in 1978, shot an atrocious thirteen on, of all holes, the thirteenth.

Tommy—a Japanese professional whose given name is Tsuneyuki, which means "always happy"—was anything but that after his second-round disaster on the 475-yard, par-five thirteenth. At the time, he was still very much in the hunt, at four under, only two shots from the lead held by Greg Norman.

"I promised myself to make an eagle on the hole," Nakajima recalled years later. "But I tried too hard and messed up."

On the slight dogleg, Nakajima tried to cut the corner with his tee shot. But his drive caught a branch and dropped into Rae's Creek, which snakes along the left side of the woods bordering the fairway. After his penalty drop, he played a five iron to within one hundred yards of the green. But then adversity struck again. He sent a weak wedge shot into the creek that fronted the green.

The ball, lying in about six inches of water, was playable. Attempting to blast out, Nakajima popped the ball up into the air, and it fell back down—right on his foot. Now he was saddled with two more penalty strokes.

"Well," he thought, "it can't get any worse." Oh, but it did. Shaken by his troubles, Nakajima tried to give his now muddy wedge to his caddie to clean. But the pair muffed the handoff and the club tumbled into the water. For grounding a club in a hazard, Nakajima incurred another two-stroke penalty. At this point, even though he had taken four shots on the hole, he was lying nine.

"By now I am confused and upset," he recalled. "I'm in the hazard, and I've just ground my club. That's two more penalty strokes. I try again and hit it over the green and into a bunker." He shook his head. "I don't like to recall unpleasant experiences. That's as far as I can remember."

But others who witnessed the debacle can never forget it. Tommy—his spirit all but crushed—blasted onto the green to within ten feet of the cup. Then he two-putted for his record-setting thirteen.

When he left the scorer's tent, Nakajima was asked by reporters how he felt. He replied in broken English that wasn't immediately understood.

"Did he say he lost his confidence?" a newsman asked Nakajima's interpreter.

"No," came the reply. "He said he lost count."

It took another eight years before Nakajima got even with the thirteenth. At the 1986 Masters, he finally eagled the hole. After splitting the fairway, he reached the green on his second shot with a five wood. Then he sank a twenty-five-footer for his eagle.

"The hole is my friend now," he said. "I feel I have more than redeemed myself for that bad day."

Mean Greens

Reuters / Corbis-Bettmann / Gary Hershorn

Germany's Bernhard Langer cries out in anguish as his must-make six-foot par putt slides by the cup.

THE MISS

Bernhard Langer
1991 Ryder Cup

Talk to the pros, and many of them will tell you that no player in the history of golf faced a more pressure-packed putt than Bernhard Langer.

It was the last match, the last hole, and the last shot of the 1991 Ryder Cup at Kiawah Island, South Carolina. Langer stood over a six-footer. If he made it, the European team would retain the Cup. If he missed it, the Americans would regain the trophy that had been kept on the other side of the Atlantic since 1985.

The six-time Ryder Cup member and winner of twenty-four European tour events had experienced the tension and strain of trying to sink the final putt for victory many times. But this was different. This was not for himself; it was for an entire continent.

Langer struck his putt—and then watched in agony when it slid by the hole. The Europeans had lost the Cup.

"I guess I will always be remembered as the guy who missed the putt that lost the Ryder Cup," Langer said a few years later. "All I can say is that I tried my best, played extremely well to get into that position, and I feel it's unfair to blame one guy."

No one on his team ever blamed him. They couldn't. They were glad they weren't in the position to attempt that putt. Even his opponent, Hale Irwin, shuddered at the thought. "I would never wish what happened on eighteen on anyone," Irwin admitted.

Patriotic fervor and boiling emotions swept over the windy Ocean Course at the twenty-ninth biennial Ryder Cup, which was billed as the "War by the Shore." The twelve-man U.S. squad was determined to return the sixty-four-year-old trophy to American soil, while the Europeans were just as determined to keep it. Making it even more of a grudge match, the Americans were peeved by the Englishmen's boast that Europe led the world in golf.

The teams were so evenly matched that they were deadlocked 8½–8½ going into Sunday's finale. It turned into a dramatic day of eleven singles matches that, as the *Los Angeles Times* said, "caused millionaires to choke, both emotionally and otherwise, and produced enough tears to make waves in the Atlantic."

Europe held a slender lead until Fred Couples beat Sam Torrance, three and two, to knot the score at 13–13. Then an emotional Lanny Wadkins closed out Mark James on the sixteenth hole to give the United States its first lead of the day. When Wadkins walked off the course, he was close to tears and unable to talk to reporters. "That's only happened to me once before, and that was at the 1983 Ryder Cup," said Wadkins after he regained his composure. "I'm a pretty vocal guy, so talking isn't usually a problem. That just shows you how much this means to everybody on this team."

With the U.S. up 14–13, it all hinged on the outcome of the last match between three-time U.S. Open champion Hale Irwin and 1985 Masters champion Bernhard Langer. "I had a sneaky suspicion that it would come down to us because we were in the last group," Irwin recalled later.

"I did not play well the last few holes, and the pressure you feel extends beyond yourself because you are playing for your country.

"On ten, eleven, and twelve, I couldn't breathe or swallow, and, making the turn on fourteen, I could hardly hit the ball."

Irwin was up two after fourteen holes, but lost the fifteenth with a bogey. Langer halved the sixteenth by getting up and down from a bunker with a clutch six-foot putt.

On the 197-yard, par-three seventeenth, Irwin three-putted from forty feet, missing his par putt from seven feet. Langer then brought his team into a tie by saving par with a four-footer. He won the hole after employing the bizarre putting style he used to cope with the yips on short putts. He gripped both the putter and his left forearm with his right hand.

The players and captains, their wives, the officials, photographers, and most of the 25,000 spectators lined the dunes from tee to green as the two players headed toward the final hole—a 438-yard par four. The animated partisan gallery chanted "USA! USA!" Irwin then hooked his drive to the left into the crowd, but the ball rebounded toward the fairway. Langer's tee shot landed on the fairway. Next, Irwin hit a three wood to within seventy feet of the pin in the short right rough. Langer's approach landed nearby, but about fifty feet from the cup.

Trying but failing to fend off the tension, Irwin lofted a weak chip that left him thirty feet short of the hole. "I couldn't breathe, I couldn't swallow," he confessed later. "The sphincter factor was high. My disappointment after my pitch shot was so great that nobody on this team will ever know what it was like." Meanwhile, Langer chipped to within six feet of the cup.

If Irwin could roll in his long putt for par, the Cup would return to the United States. But his ball stopped two and a half feet from the hole, setting up Langer's opportunity—and misfortune. Langer conceded Irwin's putt and then focused on his own. The man who had rallied from two holes down with only four left to play was now only six feet away from being the hero of an entire continent. If he holed it, he would win his match and earn his team the point it needed to tie and thus retain the trophy for an unprecedented fourth straight time.

As *New York Times* columnist Dave Anderson wrote, "Now all the weight of the Ryder Cup was on Langer's putter. All the history since 1927 from Walter Hagen and Ted Ray, to Sam Snead and Henry Cotton, to Arnold Palmer and Peter Allis, to Jack Nicklaus and Tony Jacklin, to Tom Watson and Seve Ballesteros. All the pride of European and American golf. And all the weight of every [six-foot] putt that's makeable, but missable."

Langer's teammates and his American opponents nervously sat or knelt around the green, their eyes locked on the German who twice in his career had overcome crippling bouts of the yips. Around the world, millions of television viewers held their collective breath and watched Langer step up and stroke the putt. The ball rolled toward the hole and then slid over the right edge of the cup.

Langer straightened and grimaced as if a knife had been thrust in his back. Then he unleashed a primal scream of utter despair and anguish. While the crowd roared and groaned simultaneously, the American players leaped to their feet in unbridled joy, hugging and high-fiving each other. The U.S. had recaptured the Ryder Cup by a razor-thin score of 14½ to 13½.

Amid the exultation, Irwin warmly embraced the wooden-faced Langer, a gesture that spoke volumes for their mutual respect and sportsmanship. Langer fought back tears as he left the eighteenth green. Accompanied by his consoling teammates, he walked into the squad's trailer and then broke down in sobs, unable to accept their comforting words.

"Nobody should have that much pressure on him," European team captain Bernard Gallacher said. "Bernhard is a great player."

"No one in the world could have holed that putt," declared Langer's teammate, Seve Ballesteros. "Jack Nicklaus wouldn't have holed it, nor would [former captain] Tony Jacklin. And I certainly wouldn't have holed it."

Michael Bonallack, the secretary of the Royal & Ancient, later described it as "the greatest pressure putt in the history of golf."

In the days that followed the Ryder Cup, sportswriters everywhere were hinting that "the miss" would haunt Langer for a lifetime and derail his brilliant career. He wasted little time in proving them dead wrong.

The very next week, he flew to Stuttgart, where he played splendidly at the German Masters, one of Europe's most prestigious events. He coolly made a heart-stopping fifteen-foot putt on the seventy-second hole to force a play-off, which he then won.

Looking back years later on his infamous Ryder Cup putt, Langer told Sal Maiorana of the Gannett News Service, "In the end, it was only a missed putt. I tried to do my best and that's all I can do. The world goes on, and there're far more important issues than who wins the Ryder Cup. It got blown out of proportion in a way. Obviously, I wanted to make it, and I felt bad for the team. But in the end, it's just a game, just one big tournament. There are far more important things in life.

"I struggled with it for about two or three days, then I put it behind me and that was it. Making the putt at the German Masters helped a great deal. Obviously, as I stood over that ball, I was thinking about what happened seven days earlier. But I was able to make that putt, then go on and win the play-off. That was a very big boost for the confidence.

"I came right back playing well and putting well. I was right in contention and even if I had finished second or third in the German Masters, I still played well and made a lot of putts."

Two years later at Augusta National, Langer won his second Masters title. On the European Tour, he went seventy consecutive tournaments without missing a cut.

"I've had a lot of good years," he said. "And I hope there's more to come. Sure, the putt at Kiawah could have destroyed my career. But I live in the future, not in the past."

According to a *Golf Magazine* survey among his fellow golfers, there was near unanimous agreement that if the Ryder Cup comes down to another six-foot putt, they believe the man most likely to hole it is Langer.

Langer himself is willing to give it another try. "If somebody has to be put in that position," he said, "it might as well be me."

The pressure on Bernhard Langer's Ryder Cup putt would have dissipated had American Mark Calcavecchia not choked earlier in the day. A win by Mark would have made the final match between Langer and Irwin virtually meaningless.

Playing in the third singles match, Calcavecchia, the 1989 British Open champion, was four up on Scotland's Colin Montgomerie with only four holes to play. But the pressure crimped Mark's putting stroke. He lost the fifteenth hole with a dreadful triple bogey to Colin's par. Then the American blew the sixteenth with a bogey against another par for his opponent.

Still, the rattled Calcavecchia was up by two with two holes left. It looked as if he would hang on when Montgomerie splashed his tee shot on the par-three seventeenth. But, incredibly, Mark buckled, skulling his shot so badly that it plunked into the water only halfway to the green. Even worse, Calcavecchia blew a two-foot putt for another triple bogey, giving Montgomerie the hole with a double-bogey five.

Now only one up going into the final hole, Mark was unable to recover from his devastating miscues. He bogeyed the eighteenth while Montgomerie parred it to halve the match. Instead of being down 10½ to 9½, the United States trailed 11–9.

Mark was so shattered that he fled the course in tears, hid behind a sand dune, and wept uncontrollably for fifteen minutes. "I just sat there in the sand and shook my head," he recalled. "I just needed to regroup. I cried. I lost it, mainly because I thought of the circumstances—that it might cause a loss for those other eleven guys who worked so hard."

His wife, Sheryl, then tried to console him and insisted he return to his teammates. His eyes swollen and red and his cheeks drained of color, Calcavecchia went back to the course and later watched Langer shrivel in the pressure cooker.

Said Mark, who had contributed two and a half points to the U.S. team's winning effort, "I had enough tension that week to last a lifetime."

THE PUTT THAT
MIGHT HAVE BEEN

Scott Hoch
1989 Masters

Nick Faldo won the 1989 Masters, but what most golf fans remember about the tournament is that Scott Hoch lost it—by missing a seemingly easy thirty-inch putt on the first play-off hole of sudden death.

For Scott, 1989 was a bittersweet year. On the positive side, it was his most successful after ten years on the Tour, finishing tenth on the PGA money list. But it was also the year of the putt that might have been.

In the first round of the Masters, Hoch came on late to challenge for the lead when his putter caught fire. At even par through fourteen holes, he rolled in a sixty-foot eagle putt on the fifteenth and made a twelve-footer for birdie at the eighteenth. He completed the round at sixty-nine, two shots off the pace.

The next day, Augusta's weather turned nasty. The golfers were pelted by cold rain whipped by bone-chilling twenty-five-mile-per-hour gusts. Hoch battled his nerves and the elements, relying on his putter to get him out of several jams. He saved par with seven-foot putts on the eleventh and twelfth holes and shot seventy-four. He remained two shots back at the midway point.

The weather stayed ugly on Saturday, but Hoch managed to shoot seventy-one to climb within one shot of Ben Crenshaw, who led the pack with a three-day total of three-under 213.

Ten players were within five strokes of the leader when the final round began on a gloomy, rainy Sunday. Nick Faldo charged from five shots behind and carded a marvelous seven-under sixty-five, including a thirty-foot birdie putt on the seventeenth. With a three-under total of 283, the Englishman waited in the clubhouse for nearly an hour to see if anyone would match or beat him.

Everyone but Hoch fell by the wayside. Crenshaw and Greg Norman had a chance to tie, but they bogeyed the eighteenth.

After the fifteenth hole, Hoch discovered he was in the driver's seat. "I felt good all day," he recalled. "I figured that this must be my time. I wasn't nervous. I didn't look at the scoreboard until I birdied the

AP LaserPhoto / Bill Haber

A stunned Scott Hoch flips his putter in despair seconds after his two-and-a-half-foot putt to win the 1989 Masters skidded by the hole.

fifteenth and saw I had a one-shot lead. Then I felt it was mine." If he parred the remaining three holes, he would capture his first major.

He parred the sixteenth. But his approach on the four-hundred-yard, par-four seventeenth overshot the green. He almost holed the chip coming back, however, leaving himself a four-footer. He called on his trusty putter, which had been his savior throughout the tourney, to save him once again. But he missed his par putt.

"I hit the chip of my life, then thought I'd made the putt," Hoch recalled. "I just misread it. It usually breaks more, but I guess the green was too wet. I can't second-guess myself on that one."

The bogey left him in a tie with Faldo. Shaking off the disappointment of the seventeenth, Scott coolly parred the eighteenth for a round of sixty-nine to set up the fourth sudden-death play-off in Masters history.

The playing conditions were terrible as the two headed for the tenth tee. Although the rain had let up, the low, thick clouds had left the soggy course in near darkness.

The prospects for a Hoch victory brightened considerably after Faldo sent his approach into the bunker that guards the right front of the green. Scott then hit his approach to within thirty feet of the pin.

Faldo faced a tricky bunker shot and left the ball eight feet short. Hoch, trying hard not to think about how close he was to winning his first major, studied his putt. "I thought everything through on the first putt," he recalled recently. "The rains had left the greens slower than normal. I thought I hit a good first putt. The mistake was in hitting it past the hole where I had a downhill from two and a half feet."

Seeing that Scott had an easy par putt, Faldo knew he needed to sink his own to stay alive. But his putt missed, and he had a bogey five.

A tap-in for Hoch and the title would be his. It was a putt that weekend duffers would love to have, one that doesn't require much thought. But then, hackers aren't playing for the most prestigious title in golf, for the $200,000 first-place prize, for the millions in endorsements, for the pride of wearing the green jacket, for the right to join golfing legends.

Scott Hoch was.

Normally a fast player, Hoch carefully studied the putt from every angle, circling around the ball twice. He stepped up to the ball, then took one more look at it. Finally, he stroked the ball firmly—and then watched in stunned dismay as it rolled wide left a good four feet past the hole.

Scott tossed his club up in the air in anguish and, then, without taking nearly as much time as he did with his first putt, knocked the ball dead center into the cup for bogey to continue the match.

Recalled Hoch, "I stood over that first putt and said, 'This is for all the marbles. Hit it firm.' I couldn't believe it didn't go in. I looked at it longer than normal, and there was a split second of indecision on my part before I putted it. I saw it one way, then putted it another. The message between my brain and my hands got crisscrossed. It was a poor effort on my part.

"People say I thought about the second putt too much, but that's not true. I thought about it, but not too much. Everything felt right. I felt good, and, yeah, the putt felt good. I tried to hit it firm with a break, but I missed. I just hit it too hard. The tournament was mine to win, and I missed the putt. It was something a lot of people could relate to. I hadn't three-putted all week until then."

Faldo later sympathized over Scott's misfortune. "It's a tough feeling to stand over a putt and know the world's looking at you to knock it in," said Nick. "I think he probably tried to baby it in, and he missed it. I was just standing there quietly and wondering what might happen."

Given an unexpected reprieve, the relieved Faldo split the fairway with his drive on the par-four eleventh. Then he hit a three iron onto the green twenty-five feet from the cup. After a decent drive, Hoch missed the green to the right, leaving him with a long pitch shot. Scrambling for his life, Scott hit an outstanding chip that headed directly toward the pin, but came up six feet short.

"I had visions of Larry Mize and his winning chip [in the 1987 Masters]," Hoch said afterward. "I hit it right on line, but the green was slower than we usually play it."

Gunning for a birdie and the win, Faldo then whacked his twenty-five-footer straight into the cup. He stared in disbelief for a second and then raised both arms in triumph. Hoch could only watch with his heart aching, knowing he had come within two and a half feet of becoming the joyous victor. He had to suffer the bitter frustration of seeing the green jacket that he should have won draped around the shoulders of his play-off foe.

After leaving the course, the crushed Hoch turned to his five-year-old son, Cameron, and said, "C'mon over here. Daddy needs a hug."

The golfer picked up his little boy and carried him to the clubhouse. When Scott got inside, he slammed his visor against the wall in frustration.

"Why did you do that, Daddy?" asked Cameron.

"Because I goofed up," replied Hoch, who two years earlier had missed getting into a play-off in the PGA Championship after three-putting from eight feet on the final hole.

"Daddy, did you goof up again?" Cameron innocently asked.

"Boy," replied Hoch with a pained smile, "you really know how to hurt a guy."

Scott didn't get much sympathy from the press either.

When Hoch talked to reporters immediately after the tournament, he told them, "It's a good thing I don't carry a gun."

The next day, *Chicago Tribune* columnist Bob Verdi caustically wrote,

"Not to worry. If he'd pulled the trigger like he jerked at that putt, he'd have missed and nailed a gallery marshal." (Hoch laughed when he read it and later told Verdi it was a funny line.)

Hoch's fellow golfers felt his anguish and sympathized with him.

"Some of them were good friends who came up to me and offered sympathy," Hoch said. "Other people didn't know what to say. And then there was a third category of people I didn't know very well who saw me coming and kind of went the other way, trying to avoid the whole situation."

Hoch said that when he bumped into Faldo the following week at the Heritage, their conversation was strained.

"I was looking at the starting times, and he came up trying to be friendly," Hoch recalled. "But he's not real good at that. He said, 'How are you doing?' I said, 'Well, I guess as good as can be expected. But, you know, it's kind of tough sleeping.'

"He said, 'Yeah, I know what you're talking about. I've had all these interviews. I had to get up and do *Good Morning America* and all these other things. Yeah, I know what you mean.'

"I'm just biting my lip trying not to say anything other than 'Nick, I don't think that's quite the same.' But he tried, he really did. [Craig] Stadler was standing right there, and he saw the look on my face. After Nick left, Craig said, 'Look, he just doesn't know what to say.'

"And that's right. There's nothing he could ever say that would make a difference."

Although he has yet to win a major (through 1997), the missed putt didn't traumatize Hoch. Soon after his Masters loss, Scott defeated Robert Wrenn in a nail-biting play-off to win the Las Vegas Invitational.

Nevertheless, it took Hoch nearly a year before he could bring himself to look at a videotape of the telecast of that fateful day. For four hours, he watched himself play a steady round of golf, faltering only on the seventeenth with the bogey—and then on the first hole of sudden death. The following year at the Masters, he tied for fourteenth. Faldo won it again.

For years, Hoch heard and read that his missed putt was a choke job ("Hoch as in choke"), that the pressure became so overwhelming it froze his hands. But he insists that wasn't the case.

"I didn't yip it," he declared. "After watching it several times on TV, I feel like I just lined it up wrong. It felt like a good stroke. I remember I putted it, and I felt good about it immediately. But by the time I looked up, it was missing the hole."

The miss numbed his mind. To this day, Hoch claims, he can't remember lining up and making the difficult come-backer. But he can never forget the missed putt.

"As it was explained to me by a psychologist, the way your mind works is you have long-term memory about bad things and short-term memory about good things. It's a lot easier for bad things to stay in your mind than good ones."

The press has a tendency to stress the negative, Hoch added.

"If I had lost it [the Masters] at seventeen and not made the play-off, nothing would ever have been written about the miss. But because I did what I had to do and got in the play-offs and then missed a thirty-inch putt at the tenth, with cameras right behind me, well . . .

"I didn't feel bad for myself. I felt bad for my family and my friends. I wanted to win for them, too."

He knows he may never again have such an opportunity to win a major, but he says he can accept that. "I've got to feel that it must have been in my best interest that it [a Masters victory] didn't happen. Sometimes something like this makes you a better person in the long run. Golf isn't everything in life. Sure, it was a big tournament, and it might have set me up for life. But then again, it might have made me complacent. I've just got to feel that it happened, in the long run, for the good.

"I've been a good player, but I don't get credit for what I've done. People seem to forget that I'm in the top fifteen of the all-time money winners. But I've never won a major—and that, and missing the putt at Augusta, is the thing people always talk about. It would be nice to be noticed for what you've done, not for what you haven't done. Most people feel they'd like to get what they're due, both monetarily and personally. I wonder sometimes how things would be different had I dropped that putt. More contracts? More respect? I think maybe.

"I've really had a successful career. But for a lot of people, it always comes back to missing that two-and-a-half-footer at the tenth hole."

Hubert Green knows exactly how Hoch feels. Green let his best chance at winning the 1978 Masters slip through his fingers when he failed to sink a two-and-a-half-foot birdie putt on the final hole.

Green, who had won the previous year's U.S. Open, led the field by three heading into the final round of the Masters. But Gary Player zoomed from seven strokes back to the top of the leader board with a blistering, record-tying sixty-four for an eight-under 277.

After he finished his round, Player had to sweat it out, waiting to see how his pursuers would finish. Three had a chance to tie him on the eighteenth and force a sudden-death play-off—if only they could make their birdie putts. First, defending champion Tom Watson watched his twelve-footer die just inches above the hole. Then Rod Funseth made a valiant effort from twenty-four feet. His ball trickled down the slope, but never broke and stopped directly beside the right side of the cup, a gut-wrenchingly scant two inches away.

Now Green stepped up. Those in the know figured that he would definitely make the two-and-a-half-foot putt. After all, he was considered one of the best putters on the Tour. Besides, he hadn't choked in the final round, having shot par through seventeen holes. Many spectators were beginning to gather on the first and second greens in anticipation of a play-off.

Faced with one of the biggest pressure putts in Masters history, Green examined the line from the front, side, and back. He addressed the ball and then backed off, looking up, with an annoyed expression, at the radio booth beside the green. He glared at CBS sportscaster Jim Kelly, who immediately stopped talking. A hush fell over the gallery.

Green again prepared to putt. He had a firm stroke, but pushed it ever so slightly to the right and missed. Hubert glared dejectedly at the ball and tapped it in for a par. There would be no play-off. A jubilant Gary Player had won his third Masters title, becoming, at age forty-two, the oldest golfer to win at Augusta National.

"I'm glad we didn't have a play-off," he told reporters afterward. "I'm scared of sudden death because I've lost seventeen of them."

Meanwhile, a disappointed Green was taking stock of himself. "I was pretty cocky back then and playing pretty good," he recalled recently. "I went out thinking, 'Man, I'm gonna take names and kick fannies.' After that day, I said, 'Man, I could kick my own.'

"I played just about as well as anybody had for those four days. I wish

I'd have made my putt and Gary had missed his [fifteen-footer for birdie] on eighteen, but that's all."

Added Hubert, who would later win the 1985 PGA Championship, "My father taught me to do the best you can do, then leave it behind and keep looking ahead."

THE BIG WHIFF

Hale Irwin
1983 British Open

Since turning professional in 1968, Hale Irwin has racked up twenty Tour victories, including three U.S. Open titles (1974, 1979, and 1990).

During that span, he has drained countless pressure putts, especially during the 1990 U.S. Open. Hale sank an amazing forty-five-footer on the final hole to force a play-off with Mike Donald at Medinah. Then Irwin ended the grueling nineteen-hole play-off by nailing a ten-foot birdie putt, making him, at the age of forty-five, the oldest winner ever of the Open.

But despite his brilliant greensmanship over the years, the tap-in he will never forget is the one he blew at Royal Birkdale. To put it more accurately, Hale didn't miss the tap-in—he missed the *ball!* And it cost him a chance to win the 1983 British Open.

"Everyone has an embarrassing moment, and this one is mine," Irwin admitted.

Buoyed by his victory at the Memorial Tournament earlier in the year, Hale showed up at Royal Birkdale near Southport, England, knowing that Tom Watson was the man to beat. In the previous eight years, Tom Terrific had won four British Open titles (Carnoustie, 1975; Turnberry, 1977; Muirfield, 1980; and Royal Troon, 1982). In the then 123-year history of the event, only four players had won more (Harry Vardon, six; J. H. Taylor, James Braid, and Peter Thomson, five).

Watson arrived carrying a brown box that contained the Open trophy he had won the year before. He handed the trophy back to Keith Mackenzie, secretary of the Royal & Ancient Golf Club of St. Andrews, and said, "I plan to take it back with me at the end of this week."

When Irwin heard what Tom had said, he reportedly muttered, "Not if I can help it."

At the halfway point, Irwin moved into fifth place, having shot sub-par rounds of sixty-nine and sixty-eight. He was three strokes behind leader Craig Stadler.

The third round proved both historic and fateful for Irwin. He remained among the front-runners as he reached the 198-yard, par-three

"Everyone has an embarrassing moment, and this one is mine," admits Hale Irwin, who blew a chance to be in a play-off at the 1983 British Open after whiffing on a two-inch tap-in.

fourteenth. Although he hadn't made any mistakes in the round, he hadn't gained any ground. He needed to fire up a rally and knew this hole could be the start.

His tee shot landed about twenty-five feet from the pin. After carefully reading the green, he sent his birdie try on its way. For a brief moment, the ball looked as if it would drop, but at the last moment it strayed about two inches wide.

Irwin shook his head in disappointment and then walked up to the ball. He decided to tap it in with a casual backhand stroke of his two-sided putter just as he had done hundreds of times before. Holding his putter with both hands and hitting left-handed, Irwin inexplicably looked up just as he began the stroke. The putter hit the ground behind the ball and bounced right over it. The club never touched the ball.

Incredibly, Hale had whiffed on his putt!

"It was one of those times when I just went into a momentary coma," Irwin recalled years later. "Certainly it was as much a shock to everyone else as it was to me.

"It really wasn't something done in anger. There are times that I wish it had been out of anger because it would have made it easier to justify. Maybe it's more embarrassing that it wasn't done in anger.

"As I recall, the day was sort of overcast and dark—one in which my depth perception goes off just a little bit because of my visual problems. At least, that's the story I'm going to stick to anyway.

"I misjudged just where the ball was and hit the ground behind the ball and bounced my putter up and over the ball. I had an air ball. That was the first time I'd ever done anything like that. And I can tell you it will be the last time."

At first, the crowd didn't react to what the British call an "air stroke." Recalled Hale, "I don't think a lot of people there even knew I had made a swipe at it. But I did, and where there is intent to make a stroke, it is a stroke played."

After missing a birdie by a couple of inches, Irwin walked off the green with an embarrassing bogey. It rankled him, but he shook it off by the time he teed off on the next hole. Nevertheless, he hoped the wasted stroke wouldn't play much of a factor in the final outcome.

But Fate wouldn't let this flub go to waste as just another forgettable miscue remembered only by the victim. No way.

Because of the bogey on the fourteenth, Irwin finished the third round at one-over seventy-two. At four under for the tournament, he was now tied for seventh place, four strokes behind the new leader, Tom Watson.

The next day, Irwin tried not to think about the whiff. But it wasn't easy, not after he began to make his move. At the turn in the final round, Hale was one of four golfers at six under, one stroke behind leaders Nick Faldo and Graham Marsh.

Faldo and Marsh, however, faltered down the stretch, leaving the door open for Watson, Lee Trevino, Irwin, and his playing partner, Andy Bean, to take control.

Trevino took himself out by bogeying the eighteenth to finish at six under. Playing ahead of Watson, Irwin birdied the thirteenth and seventeenth and parred the other holes on the back nine to go eight under and grab a share of the lead with Bean. Then the two sat in the clubhouse and waited for Watson, who was also at eight under with three holes to play.

At the 415-yard, par-four sixteenth, Watson cracked a perfect three wood into the fairway, dropped an eight iron to within twenty feet of the pin, and holed the putt for a birdie. Now he was nine under and had regained the lead. He was two pars away from victory. After Tom scrambled at the 526-yard, par-five seventeenth to make par, he faced the 473-yard, par-four eighteenth, a dogleg right that he had parred in the three previous rounds.

After a picture-perfect drive, Watson sent his two iron eighteen feet past the pin. He had two putts to win.

Back in the clubhouse, where many of the players were watching the finish on television, Irwin relived his third-round air ball. He turned to a couple of reporters and confessed, "I know I made an error yesterday which is a very critical error. It looms rather large now, doesn't it? I really don't know what happened. I'm guessing I had a mental lapse.

"I'm going to look at Tom on television. I'm hoping he takes just one putt. If he takes two, I'm going to kick myself all the way home."

On the green, Watson wasn't about to take any unnecessary chances. He lagged his approach putt perfectly and then tapped the ball in to lay claim to his fifth British Open title.

Irwin finished in a tie for second, thanks to his mortifying third-round whiff.

At the post-tournament interview, Irwin told reporters, "Don't make more of it [the blown putt] than it really was. It's history. How can you say it cost me the British Open? Who knows whether I would have beaten Tom in a play-off?

"The whiff was nothing more than any other error, much like a ball out of bounds."

"Yes, in terms of numbers on the scorecard, you're right," said a reporter. "But weighed on the scales, a missed two-inch putt somehow seems heavier."

Years later, Irwin admitted the significance of that pitiful putt. "Yes, it ultimately cost me a chance at the title. It didn't hurt that much at the time I did it. It was just like another shot you may have hit into the water or topped the ball or hit any number of bad shots during the course of a tournament. You say to yourself, 'Why did I do that? Why couldn't I have done better?' This was certainly carelessness.

"I don't dwell on it nearly as much as I could have. Maybe it's just as well that I haven't. I block it out pretty well until I get asked about it and have to replay it over again. Then I dwell on it for a little while.

"Of course, the thing that makes it embarrassing now is that Tom won by just one stroke. Otherwise, nobody would've remembered my little air ball. Ever since, I've been very careful about my tap-ins. It was probably the most expensive putting lesson in history—at least it was for me."

You would think that after Hale Irwin's startling whiff, every pro golfer in the world would have been extra-cautious on tap-ins—at least while the incident was still fresh in their minds.

But Andy Bean—Irwin's playing partner at the British Open—needed another tournament to learn that same lesson.

Just two weeks after the "air stroke," Bean suffered his own careless mishap on a simple tap-in with similar devastating consequences. It happened on the fifteenth green in the third round of the Canadian Open at the Glen Abbey Golf Club near Toronto.

Bean was facing almost the identical two-inch putt for par that Irwin had at Royal Birkdale. Being lazy, cute, or absentminded, Bean tapped the ball in with the *grip* of his putter instead of the head. Bean didn't know he was violating Rule 19, which states: "The ball shall be fairly struck at with the head of the club and must not be pushed, scraped or spooned." A PGA Tour official, who saw the goofy stroke on television and recognized it as an infraction, alerted tourney officials.

When word reached Bean on the course, he had to change his score to reflect the two-stroke penalty that was assessed against him. The infraction raised Andy's score for the round from seventy-five to seventy-seven.

Although he was irritated with himself, Bean didn't think much of the gaffe because at the time of the incident he seemed out of contention. But it became significant in the final round, when he shot a record-tying sixty-two and finished the tournament at a five-under 279.

For nearly three hours, Bean, an early starter, waited in the clubhouse to see if his score would hold up. Unfortunately for Andy, John Cook and Johnny Miller were tied at seven under at the end of the day and went into a play-off, which Cook won. Bean was two strokes shy of joining them in the play-off, the measure of his penalty.

"What can I say?" Bean told reporters afterward. "It was a dumb thing to do—and I paid for it."

Head Cases

His face a picture of determination and boldness, Jesper Parnevik attacks the final hole of the 1994 British Open, wrongly thinking he needs a birdie.

AP Photo / Doug Ball

LOOKING THE OTHER WAY

Jesper Parnevik
1994 British Open

It was what Jesper Parnevik wouldn't do that cost him a shot at the 1994 British Open title. He wouldn't look at the scoreboard on the back nine.

As a result, when he reached the final hole, he didn't realize he was ahead and in control of his own destiny. Wrongly thinking he had to birdie the eighteenth to tie what was really a phantom front-runner, Jesper played too aggressively and wound up with a bogey and a second-place finish.

To those who know Jesper well, it was no surprise that he would do something bizarre like that.

They fondly call him "Spaceman," but not because his head is a void. In fact, it's just the opposite. He is an intellectual who can discuss a fascinating array of topics from the sacred nature of the Koran (which he has read) to quantum mechanics (which he has studied). He speaks three languages (Swedish, English, and German), is a math wiz, and can memorize a list of over one hundred items in only a few minutes.

His mind is so full it seems he has little room for the mundane. He once lost his plane ticket four times during a single trip—he left one in the hotel room and another on his discarded lunch tray during a flight, dropped the third in the crack between the computer and the airline agent's desk during a layover, and never did know what happened to the fourth.

More than once he has driven away from a golf course while his clubs stayed behind in the parking lot, that is, when he didn't mislay his car keys. One time, for a Swedish tournament, he drove to the wrong city. At least twice, at tournaments, he forgot what hotel he was staying at.

"I've done a lot of spacey things," Parnevik admits. "All my life people have been telling me I have talent, but I think they might be a little surprised when I succeed because I've always done so many dumb things."

So far in his golfing career, his decision not to look at the leader board during the final round of the 1994 British Open has been his dumbest.

The Swedish-born golfer—the son of Bo Parnevik, the most famous comedian in Sweden—was thirteen when he first announced that he would one day win the British Open. As a teen, he practiced his swing by hitting floating golf balls into the lake behind his home. He quickly rose through the Swedish national golf program and turned pro at the age of twenty-one in 1986. Two years later he qualified for the European Tour. After winning the 1993 Scottish Open, he joined the PGA Tour in 1994, finishing fifth at the United Airlines Hawaiian Open in his first PGA event.

Several months later, Jesper entered the British Open at Turnberry in Scotland. Adding to his reputation as a Swedish meatball, Parnevik wore his golf cap with the brim up, Gomer Pyle–style, as if he were playing in a hurricane. (He has worn his cap that way ever since he turned up the cap bill to get some sun and played a terrific round.)

Despite his image as a flake, Parnevik impressed many at Turnberry. He shot sixty-eight in rainy, windy weather in the first round followed by sixty-six, leaving him one stroke behind leader Tom Watson at the midway point. Jesper then fired his third straight subseventy round, this time sixty-eight. As the final round began, Parnevik was one of four golfers who trailed coleaders Fuzzy Zoeller and Brad Faxon by a stroke. Joining Parnevik at 202 were Tom Watson, Nick Price, and Ronan Rafferty.

At the turn of the final round on the Ailsa Course, the leaders were struggling. Parnevik, who had scored nothing but pars through the tenth hole, then made his move—and a fateful decision. "I made up my mind on the back nine that I wasn't going to look at the scoreboards," Parnevik recalled. "I was just going to play."

On the eleventh hole, he struck a solid six iron to within six feet of the cup and sank it for his first birdie of the day. Although he didn't know it, Jesper had taken over the lead for the first time at nine under.

He then walloped a nice drive into the twelfth fairway and followed with an eight iron that flew dead on line at the flagstick, stopping six feet short. He drained that putt for another birdie and now pulled ahead by two strokes.

Parnevik split the thirteenth fairway and sent his approach to within four feet of the cup. He knocked in his third straight birdie putt to go eleven under. But he failed to pull farther away from his pursuers because Price birdied the twelfth and Zoeller the eleventh. Both of them were now at nine under.

Jesper parred the fourteenth but bogeyed the fifteenth when he missed the green, which cut his lead to a single stroke. Meanwhile, right behind him, Price scrambled to save par on the thirteenth and fourteenth holes with, respectively, a nerveless pitch and a running seven iron, both stopping about four feet from the cup to the roars of the crowd.

Still not knowing he was in the lead, Parnevik birdied the sixteenth with a fifteen-footer and birdied the seventeenth hole after an impressive pitch-and-run stopped four feet from the cup.

He was now at twelve under. The championship was his for the taking, but he didn't know it. Even though scoreboards were everywhere, Jesper refused to take a peek at any of them. All he knew for sure was his score, which he didn't think would be good enough to win, especially after hearing roars erupting from the gallery at the holes behind him. Those cheers were for hard-won pars, but Parnevik assumed the yells were for birdies by his closest competitors.

"Every time I made a birdie, I heard screaming from the green behind me," Jesper said later. "I thought, 'This is unbelievable.' I knew they [his closest competitors] were doing well. I thought I needed a birdie at the eighteenth because I kept hearing all those roars behind me."

Believing he had to play aggressively for a birdie if he had any chance of winning, Parnevik sent his drive to the right edge of the fairway. Then, from 150 yards away, he decided to go for the flagstick with a pitching wedge. But he simply didn't have enough club. His ball dropped short and settled against a grassy bank in front of the green. "I saw [playing partner] Tom Watson's [approach] shot and it flew, so I thought I'd get a flyer," Jesper recalled. "It just didn't reach. It hit the bank and came back. Then, it was sitting pretty deep in the grass. I had to play it like a bunker shot, and it came up short."

His recovery stopped six feet from the cup, and he missed the putt to bogey the hole. Instead of the four, which, as it turned out, would have earned him a play-off spot, he made a five.

While Parnevik went into the scorer's tent with an eleven-under 269, Price reached the green on the par-five seventeenth in two. Then he ran an astounding fifty-footer into the cup for an eagle that vaulted him into the lead, a stroke ahead of Parnevik. Price parred the final hole with a gritty, pressure-filled two-putt to claim the British Open title with a final-round sixty-six and twelve-under total of 268.

Parnevik, who shot sixty-seven for the day, finished second.

Talking to reporters afterward, Jesper admitted, "I thought I was chasing someone else. It was a big mistake. Had I known my position, I think I would have gone for the middle of the green.

"I thought if I got to thirteen under par I would win. So when I was twelve under on the last hole, I thought I needed another birdie. When I walked off the green and saw I had a two-stroke lead, I was crushed because I should have looked at the scoreboard. The way it turned out I should've played a smarter shot.

"Some have blamed my caddie, but he thought I knew. Who wouldn't? But I was very focused on what I was doing, and just trying to birdie every hole."

Price, a veteran of twelve years on the Tour at the time and the 1992 PGA champion, knew better than to ignore the leader boards. "A lot of strategy is dictated by what the other guys are doing," he said.

Greg Norman, who has experienced more close finishes in major championships than anybody in recent years, told reporters he always looks at the scoreboard. "I like to know where I stand," he said. "But I can understand a young player not wanting to know if he's playing well and wants to be aggressive. But I bet next time, he'll peek."

Jesper does. "I always look at the scoreboard now," he said.

Although Parnevik may have blown a major championship, he now thinks he made up for it in major karma. "It was my first chance to win a major, but I didn't deserve it yet," he said recently. "It would've been too soon. Besides, in the long run, it's just your name on something, isn't it?"

In addition to picking up some karma, he also picked up some extra cash from his mental blunder. Shortly after his British Open performance, Parnevik poked fun at himself in one of Choice Hotels International's celebrity-in-a-suitcase TV commercials.

In the ad, which aired during the PGA Championship telecasts, Parnevik pops out of the suitcase. Choice's toll-free phone number is clearly visible on his hotel room walls, a mirror, his bed, his shirt, and trademark upturned cap bill. "Recently, I have had some trouble with numbers," he says in the commercial. "So I want to be completely sure of this one. To reserve a room at any Quality, Comfort, Clarion, or Sleep Hotel, anywhere in the world, call . . ." He hesitates as he looks around the room. Then he spots a cue card with the number and sheepishly says, ". . . 1–800–4–CHOICE."

If there was any doubt that Parnevik is the most eccentric player on the PGA Tour, it was erased at the 1996 Sprint International at Castle Pines, in Castle Rock, Colorado.

The tournament cuts its field to twenty-four players for the final round. Jesper was one of four players tied with fifteen points for the final spot, which calls for a sudden-death play-off. Wrongly thinking the cut was sixteen, Parnevik left the course and returned to the hotel. Once there, he learned about the play-off and rushed back to Castle Pines, only to find out the play-off had finished without him.

"I broke all speed records trying to get back," said Jesper. "It was entirely my fault."

Ernie Els
1994 U.S. Open

Jesper Parnevik should have learned from Ernie Els's experience.

A month before Parnevik's British Open mental blunder, Els ignored the huge scoreboard during the final round of the 1994 U.S. Open.

Els mistakenly thought he needed a birdie at the eighteenth to catch Loren Roberts. So he played too aggressively, got in trouble, and then had to scramble for a bogey to fall into a three-way play-off. A par would have won it for Ernie.

The only difference between Els's gaffe and Jesper's was that Ernie ultimately won, although it took him twenty extra holes to do it.

The twenty-four-year-old South African had mastered three rounds of stifling heat, slick greens, and shaggy rough at Oakmont Country Club, outside Pittsburgh, for a three-stroke lead over four pursuers. Starting the final round at seven under, Els bogeyed the first and sixteenth holes, dropping him into a tie with Roberts.

Hearing gallery cheers for the group in front of him, Ernie refused to look at the scoreboard to find out what was happening. He just assumed he needed a birdie on one of the last two holes to win. Els tried to drive the green at the seventeenth but failed and settled for a par.

Meanwhile, up ahead on the eighteenth, Roberts faced a four-foot par putt that would have won the tournament. It was exactly the kind of putt he had been making all week, uphill with a slight right to left break. But with the Open on the line, he opened the blade of his putter and pushed the putt to the right. He took a bogey five.

"I hit a terrible putt," Roberts told the press later. "The ball didn't roll for me because I hit it so bad." He admitted the pressure got to him. "I'm not going to lie to you, I had trouble taking the putter back."

At the eighteenth tee, Els didn't know that Roberts had missed the short putt up ahead, that a par would win it. He was still thinking he needed a birdie.

Rather than play safe with a three wood or two iron into the fairway on the 452-yard hole, he took out his driver—a club he had hooked badly three times down the stretch. "I tried to smash the living stuffing out of it," he recalled. He belted it so far left that it landed near the bushes by the fifteenth tee. Els then prepared to go for the green.

"It was kind of an impossible shot," he recalled. "From a scale of one to ten, I had a chance of about three of hitting the green. It would have been a miracle, a Seve Ballesteros kind of shot. Then my caddie said, 'Whoa, whoa, look at the scoreboard. You're one shot ahead.'"

Els laughed as he recounted the moment. "If I hadn't listened to him,

I might still be thrashing away." Ernie chipped out into a sandy divot and left his third shot forty-five feet from the hole. He lagged up to within four feet—just where Roberts had missed from—and knocked it in for a sweat-drenched bogey five. It was one too many strokes to avoid a play-off with Roberts and Colin Montgomerie.

"If I had known I needed a par, I would have hit an iron off the tee," Els said. "I just didn't look at the scoreboard."

Smarting from his oversight, Els began the next day with a bogey and a triple bogey but recovered for a seventy-four that tied Roberts and forced just the second sudden-death play-off in Open history. They both parred the tenth, the first extra hole.

On the eleventh, Roberts's thirty-five-foot par putt hit the right lip and spun out. Ernie two-putted from eighteen feet for par and the title.

"He's a true champion because he was able to come back," said Roberts. "That's what true champions do."

Yeah, but true champions also look at the scoreboard.

And they don't talk themselves out of victory. Els admits that's exactly what he did in the final round of the 1995 PGA Championship at Riviera Country Club in Los Angeles. Els had a three-stroke lead—a tourney-record 197—going into the final round. But he stumbled and finished third, two strokes behind winner Steve Elkington.

"I've got two U.S. Opens under my belt, but that loss still haunts me," Els revealed just days after winning the 1997 U.S. Open. "Even today, two years later, I still sometimes find myself dwelling on it. You really sit and recall every shot and ask, 'What could I have done differently?'"

It wasn't so much bad shots as it was bad thoughts during the final round. Recalled Els:

"All I thought about the whole day was the word 'lose.' I stood on the tee thinking, 'Don't lose, don't lose, don't lose' instead of 'Win, win, win.' I played conservatively, and I lost. It was as simple as that. I'd been playing great golf, and then I changed my whole game plan. I began thinking about not losing instead of winning, and that mind-set, I think, cost me the PGA."

A MISTAKE OF OLYMPIC PROPORTIONS

Arnold Palmer
1966 U.S. Open

Arnold Palmer was so intent on smashing the record for the lowest score ever in the U.S. Open that he lost sight of his original goal—to win the championship.

As a result of his wayward thinking, Arnie blew a seven-shot lead over the final nine holes and wound up losing in one of the greatest collapses ever in a major tournament.

The finish over the hilly, tree-lined Olympic Country Club Course in San Francisco was as unexpected as it was dramatic. Starting the day with a three-stroke lead, Palmer fired a nifty three-under thirty-two on the front nine to go up by seven at the turn over Billy Casper. Arnie was on a pace to shatter the then Open record of 276 set by Ben Hogan in 1948 at Riviera in Los Angeles. Palmer needed to shoot a one-over thirty-six to break the mark.

Hardly anyone gave Casper a chance of catching Arnie. Even after a bogey on the tenth and another on the thirteenth, Palmer still had a seemingly safe five-stroke lead. All he had to do was make par the rest of the way to break Hogan's record and, barring a miraculous all-birdie finish by Casper, capture the title.

But then, after a par on the fourteenth, Arnie's shot-making skills disappeared into the golf world's Bermuda Triangle.

His seven-iron tee shot on the 150-yard fifteenth fell into a bunker. He blasted out to within eight feet from the pin, but missed the putt, taking a bogey four. Casper knocked in a twenty-footer for a birdie, leaving Palmer only three ahead.

Arnie gave no thought to playing safe. He disregarded layup tee shots and middle-of-the-green approaches. And the strategy cost him dearly.

The 604-yard, par-five sixteenth proved the turning point. Instead of laying up with a three wood, he pulled out his driver. "Hitting a three wood is for someone else, not me," he once said. He duck-hooked his tee shot, which hit a tree, skimmed off a branch, and fell into the rough just 180 yards from the tee. Arnie tried to muscle a three iron out of the tangled rough and dribbled the ball only a few yards away. He then used a nine iron to get back onto the fairway. From there, he smashed a three wood that traveled into the right bunker. Arnie blasted out to within four feet and sank the putt for a bogey six. "The greatest six I ever had," he later said with a trace of sarcasm.

Meanwhile, Casper rolled in an eighteen-foot putt for a birdie four. Palmer, whose lead had seemed insurmountable a few holes back, now had only one stroke to spare with two holes left to play.

But his thin margin disappeared on the seventeenth. He drove into the rough again, on the left side of the fairway. Then the face of his six iron turned on his second shot and the ball scooted to the right rough. From there he hit a wedge to within seven feet of the flagstick. The putt didn't go down, and Palmer had his third straight bogey. Casper drilled a five-footer for par to tie Arnie.

On the 337-yard, par-four eighteenth, Palmer sent his drive into deep rough. Staving off defeat, Arnie made a courageous nine-iron shot up to the small, guarded green. His twenty-five-foot, downhill birdie putt was short. But he sank a tricky six-foot downhill, left to right, that he later claimed "at the time was the biggest putt in my life."

After missing a seventeen-footer for a birdie, Billy tapped in for par. The shell-shocked Palmer walked off the green, knowing he faced an eighteen-hole play-off the next day.

Before his collapse, most everyone assumed Palmer would break Hogan's scoring record. Unfortunately, Arnie began to think so, too.

"Maybe that was my mistake," he admitted to reporters after the round. "I should have known that on this course you must keep your game together. I tried for shots that are great when they work. If they don't, you're in trouble. I was in trouble."

Wrote famed *New York Times* sports columnist Arthur Daley, "Not since the fourth game of the 1929 World Series [when the Chicago Cubs blew an 8–0 seventh-inning lead and lost 10–8 to the Philadelphia Athletics] has there been such a violent turnabout in a major sports event.

"What sets [Palmer] apart from the other divot-diggers is that he is invariably willing to gamble on the impossible—or the near impossible anyway. Especially on the 15th and 16th holes yesterday, he took risks that he never should have taken. They cost him dearly . . . Arnie's boldness is sometimes his undoing.

"When he was going like gangbusters on the first nine, he somehow lost sight of his main objective. He began to dream of breaking Hogan's record of 276 for the tournament. When Arnie reached the 15th tee, the start of his unwinding, he needed only pars the rest of the way to gain the record. In a similar situation, Hogan would have dismissed the record from his mind and made sure that he won the championship.

AP Wirephoto

Arnold Palmer grimaces with pain as his birdie putt at fourteen re-
fuses to fall—part of his monumental collapse at the 1966 U.S. Open.

The chief requirement for rabbit pie still is this: first catch the rabbit. Arnie let him escape."

The next day, Palmer looked like his old self, moving out to a two-stroke lead at the turn with two birdies—a thirty-three to Casper's even-par thirty-five. But, once again, Arnie faltered on the back nine.

On the eleventh, Casper holed a thirty-footer for a birdie. Palmer hit his second shot from the rough to the left of the green and failed to get a four-footer down. His tap-in for a bogey five left him in a tie.

After they both parred the twelfth, Casper went ahead for the first time by running in a forty-footer for a birdie on the thirteenth. Appearing slightly rattled, Arnie sent his drive on the fourteenth into the rough. He bogeyed the hole, while Billy parred it to take a two-stroke lead.

Casper widened the gap to three strokes on the fifteenth after Palmer was bunkered and took another bogey. Arnie never recovered. His torture ended on the eighteenth when, after his drive hit a policeman in the leg, Palmer scrambled to save par while Casper drained a birdie putt, giving him a round of sixty-nine and the title. Palmer ballooned to a forty on the back nine for a seventy-three.

"I was certainly very disappointed to lose the Open at Olympic, but it made me a lot better," Palmer said recently. "It told me something about the fans and the people who supported me over all the years I had played. The incredible part was that the fans and my friends gave me greater support after that loss than they would had I won. They didn't desert me."

He said the receptions he received in the weeks and months after the debacle were warmer and bigger.

"It wasn't just a feeling of sympathy, which I would not have liked. It was more the fact that I had lost, and that happens. I took the positive side rather than the negative. From the personal side, it was fine."

Palmer insists that on the competitive side, he came to terms with the potentially crushing loss.

"A couple of things happened that made it less painful," he said. "Bill played awfully good golf. What the hell. It wasn't just a situation of my bobbling it. That was important. Plus, I made a couple of shots and pressure putts that kept me from losing in the final round. I don't know if that was important to anybody else, but it was important to me."

He mentioned the nine iron he whacked out of thick rough on the eighteenth and a downhill five-foot par putt on that hole to force the play-off.

Although Palmer won twelve more times on the PGA Tour, he never captured another major. Asked if his stunning defeat affected his play, Arnie replied, "Not really. Certainly I remembered things like Olympic . . . But if you go over almost anyone's career that has been a golfer of some note, you are going to find those situations. You have to put it behind you. You'd better do that if you want to win again. It's that simple. You can sit and reminisce and talk about losing and why you lost, but if you let it get to you on the golf course, you're in trouble."

In the enjoyable book *Arnie: Inside the Legend* by *Orlando Sentinel* columnist Larry Guest, Palmer recalled that at the turn in the final round, Casper seemed less concerned about trailing Arnie by seven strokes and more worried about Jack Nicklaus who was two strokes behind Billy.

Palmer recalled, "Bill walked over to me as we headed down the tenth fairway, and he said, 'If I don't play better, Nicklaus is going to beat me for second.' He said it casually, no panic in his voice—just sort of making conversation.

"I said, 'Don't worry. If I can help you, I will.' I didn't mean it in a cheating way. It was just a friendly way, or moral support. Well, I did help him. I helped him win the tournament.

"At the turn, I never thought of losing the golf tournament or even thought it was humanly possible. But it was, as I found out. I suppose there was some point when I began to think I could lose the tournament, and that was the bad part. I never did really get defensive. I kept going strong all the way. If I had gotten a little defensive, I might have won."

From Casper's point of view, Palmer made a very un-Palmer-like mistake. "At first, Arnold was thinking about Hogan's record," Casper told Guest. "Then when that slipped away and I started gaining on him, he panicked. I've played with Arnold a lot, and that's the first time I've ever seen him . . . choke. He couldn't make a swing. Everything was a pull hook."

Guest once asked Palmer if, given an opportunity to turn back the clock, what he would have done differently on the final nine to win the 1966 Open. "I would shoot thirty-eight," Arnie joked.

Turning serious, Palmer claimed he wouldn't have done it any differently. "At that point in time, the one and only thing that could have changed my situation was to make a couple of putts.

"I'll be very honest. I have never looked back at a golf tournament and said I would have changed the way I played. That's my style. That's the way I got here, and that's the way I'm gonna go out."

Arnold Palmer
1961 Masters

When pressed, Arnold Palmer will admit to a tournament in which he would change one thing if given a second chance—he wouldn't commit the mental blunder that cost him the 1961 Masters.

"There was a mistake once that I made playing golf that I felt cost me a tournament," he told Larry Guest. "I was walking up the eighteenth fairway at Augusta on the final day of the 1961 Masters. A friend called me over to the ropes and said, 'Congratulations,' and I shook hands with him. Now that was a mistake, one that I would change if I could."

Arnie held a one-stroke lead over Gary Player and needed to par the final hole to become the first golfer to win back-to-back Masters titles. The previous year, Palmer knocked in two birdies on the final two holes to nip Ken Venturi. So parring the 405-yard, par-four eighteenth this time seemed a much easier task.

"I never for one minute thought I was going to lose," Arnie recalled. The gallery didn't either.

Meanwhile, Player was in the clubhouse with an eight-under 280, wondering if he would win, lose, or prepare for a play-off.

Back on the course, Palmer hit a drive of about 260 yards, and Arnie's Army whooped with delight, convinced that the next few shots were a mere formality. As he walked up the fairway, Palmer had a brain sprain—he let friends slap him on the back in anticipation of victory. He fell victim to overconfidence.

Arnie wasn't mentally prepared for his next shot because he was in too big of a hurry to win. As a result, his approach with the seven iron tailed off in the air and dropped into the right-hand bunker. Concerned but not panicked, Palmer studied his partly buried ball. "All I had to do was splash out of the bunker, leaving me a putt for victory or two putts for a play-off with Player," he recalled.

But the crowd gasped when Palmer caught the ball thin. His recovery sailed over the green, down a nasty slope, and nestled in the grass about thirty feet from the pin. To win, he needed to hole the next shot. He tried to putt the ball back up, but it ran fifteen feet past the cup. Now he needed to sink the putt for a bogey and a play-off. The ball touched the rim of the hole, but stayed out. With his shocking double-bogey six, Palmer had just handed the title to a jubilant Gary Player.

"That was a bad mistake, one that I shouldn't have done," said Arnie. "But any other golf tournament that I lost or won, I accept the conditions in which I won or lost."

THE WRONG STICK

Lee Trevino
1970 British Open

Of all the courses in the world, Lee Trevino had to pull his greatest blunder at storied St. Andrews, the birthplace of golf, during the ninety-ninth British Open in 1970.

Although only in his third year on the PGA Tour, Trevino was out-classing his fellow golfers, having won two tournaments that year and soaring to the top of the money list.

With his smile, charm, and skill, Trevino quickly became a crowd favorite. Firing back-to-back sixty-eights, Lee jumped ahead of defending champion Tony Jacklin and 1966 winner Jack Nicklaus by a stroke at the midway point.

Things looked good for Lee until he fell victim to two bizarre situations that he had never encountered before or since in a major. Both shattered his concentration.

At the start of the third round, Lee arrived at the first tee, where he was introduced to British prime minister Edward Heath. Lee grasped Heath's hand warmly and cracked, "Ever shake hands with a Mexican?" The prime minister and the gallery roared with laughter.

Then Trevino put on his game face and stubbornly tried to protect his tenuous lead.

But his concentration failed him on the sixteenth green. Preparing to putt for par from seven feet, Trevino became irritated by a barking dog in the crowd. (Because St. Andrews is a town park, dogs were welcome.) Lee asked the owner to quiet the dog, which he did.

But just as Trevino drew back his putter, the dog barked again. Lee stabbed the putt wide and then tapped in for a bogey five. As he and caddie Willie Aitchison walked off the green, Trevino muttered, "If I'd gotten to that dog, it would have gone home with a putter in its head. Here I am playing for a million dollars—and that's what this championship is worth to me—and I've come here early and hit seven hundred balls a day and I might blow it right there because some guy is out walking his dog."

Lee Trevino remembers the anguish he felt after bogeying the fifth hole at St. Andrews. He had hit to the wrong flag on the double green— a gaffe from which he never recovered.

Lee managed to get his head back into the game of golf and parred the seventeenth. Then he banged in a twenty-five-footer for a birdie three, giving him a round of even-par seventy-two and a three-day total of eight-under 208. Going into the final eighteen holes, he now held a two-stroke lead over Nicklaus, Jacklin, and Doug Sanders.

Trevino knew he needed total concentration if he was to maintain his lead. But after three holes, in which Lee recorded a bogey while Sanders and Nicklaus made two birdies, the three were tied at seven under. Nicklaus then birdied the par-five fifth, and took the lead for the first time.

After all these years, Trevino still winces over what happened to him on the fifth hole—one of St. Andrews's famed immense double greens. Among the Old Course's unique features is a layout in which most of the holes on the front nine share common greens with most of the holes on the back nine. (There are only four single greens.) The double greens have two pins with different-colored flags—the outgoing ones are white and the incoming ones are red. The greens are so big that rarely does a ball hit by a pro come anywhere near where golfers are putting at the other cup.

Hearing the cheers of the Nicklaus-Jacklin pairing up ahead, Trevino and playing partner Sanders knew that the Golden Bear had made another birdie. Intent on trying to catch up with Jack, Lee hit two good woods on the fifth hole and was a short iron away from the green.

Not one to waste time planning a shot, Trevino considered the wind factor and then used an eight iron. He hit it well and had the ball dead on line, right toward the flag—the red one. Even though Lee had played the hole three times in the tournament, his usual alertness faded like a poor drive.

As the ball sailed toward the pin, Trevino slapped his forehead like one of the Three Stooges and yelped for all to hear, "I've done hit to the wrong stick!"

The ball was still rolling toward the pin on the thirteenth hole when he added, "It takes a dummy like me to hit a shot like that." Walking toward the thirteenth hole while his playing partner headed for the fifth, Lee shook his head and told the crowd, "I've worried about that all week long, and now I've done it."

His ball was on the green, but eighty feet away from the fifth hole. Shaken by his blunder, Lee needed three putts for a bogey six, which put him two shots behind the new leader. Trevino never recovered. He shot a disappointing seventy-seven in the final round and tied for third with Harold Henning at 285, two strokes behind coleaders Nicklaus and Sanders, who were deadlocked at five-under 283.

(Sanders had his own ignoble moment when he blew a chance to win it all on the final hole by missing a three-footer. He and Nicklaus then battled the next day in an eighteen-hole play-off that Jack won, 72–73.)

Lee eventually made up for his fifth-hole boner. The next year, he won the British Open, edging Lu Liang Huan 278–279. And just to prove that it was not a fluke, Trevino was victorious again the following year, this time beating Nicklaus by the same score.

Nick Price
1982 British Open

The British Open has been known to play tricks with golfers' heads. It lulls them into mental lapses, as it did to Lee Trevino. And it seduces them into false confidence, as it did to Nick Price.

At the 1982 British Open at Royal Troon, Nick discovered that too much confidence is as harmful as too little. Price was a brash but unheralded twenty-five-year-old with only one European Tour victory in his young career. Yet he made himself known by shadowing the surprise leader, twenty-two-year-old American Bobby Clampett, throughout each of the first three rounds.

Before the start of the final round, Nick was at four-under 212, one shot behind Clampett. "I think I can win," Price declared. "I believe in myself, and I believe I have the ability to win."

Clampett soon fell back in the pack, and Nick surged into the lead. At the turn, Price was four under, leading Tom Watson, who was playing two groups ahead of him, by one.

Price then reeled off birdies on the tenth, eleventh, and twelfth holes to go seven under. Having built a three-shot cushion with only six holes left, he was more confident than ever that victory was his. After all, in the opening round he had played the final six holes in one under when the wind and cold were at their harshest. And now on this Sunday, the sun was shining and the wind was light—perfect conditions. Besides, those finishing holes accounted for only one bogey in his previous two rounds. He was pumped. He could taste the victory champagne.

With naive cockiness, Nick turned to his caddie at the thirteenth tee and boldly announced, "Well, we've got it now." But Price soon would gag on his own words.

A poor drive and a too-short approach cost him a bogey at the thirteenth. Although this was cause for concern, Price knew he still had a two-shot lead over Watson, so he focused on the next hole, which he parred. Feeling more confident, he could see his name etched on the silver Claret Jug.

But what he eventually would see was his name on a list of British Open crash victims.

On the 457-yard, par-four fifteenth, he drove into the rough. With a four iron, he aimed for the downslope leading to the green, but the ball was deflected by a patch of long grass into a bunker. He barely made it out of the trap, twenty yards onto the fairway. His fourth shot was a poor chip twenty feet short of the pin, and from there he needed two putts.

Price had taken a double-bogey six, his only double of the entire British Open. It left him at four under and in a tie with Watson.

After parring the sixteenth, Nick faced the 223-yard, par-three seventeenth. His two iron came up short. He hit a bad chip, about eight feet long, and missed his par putt. Walking off the green with a bogey four, Price had dropped four shots in five holes—all after he had boldly told his caddie, "Well, we've got it now."

Watson, who had finished thirty minutes earlier, now had the lead. Tom came out to the green on the par-four eighteenth to see if the cocky South African could get the birdie that would send them into a play-off. After a poor drive, Nick hit a superb approach that came to rest twenty-five feet from the cup. He had to make the putt to stay alive. Before a jammed, breathless gallery, he stroked the ball solidly and watched it break left of the cup. The tournament was over. Price carded a seventy-three for the round and a three-under 285—one stroke behind Watson.

"I feel great empathy for Nick Price," Watson said afterward. "He gave me the tournament. I've never been in a position where a man has given me a tournament from so far ahead. But after ten years on the tour, I know these things happen. They've happened to me, too. I cried when they happened, but they made me a tougher player."

In the interview room, Nick admitted, "I blew this one. But I'll know enough not to blow another one. I'm going to dream about this and have nightmares. But I don't expect to be depressed after placing second in the world's greatest championship."

Those words were hollow, Price confessed years later.

"Immediately afterward, I was really depressed," he recalled. "At that stage in my life, twenty-five years old, I played well enough to win a major championship. I don't think there are too many people that age who've come that close.

"But then I worked my way out of the depression. I told myself that I had fifteen to twenty years of my career ahead of me. If I worked on the right things and analyzed my mistakes and tried to correct them, then I figured I'd be a much better golfer."

He was right. Nick became the leading money winner on the Tour in 1993 and 1994 and has won two PGA Championships (1992 and 1994) and the British Open (1994).

"Maybe it helped me not to win the British Open in 1982," he said. "Maybe if I'd won it, I would've thought, 'Hey, I've got all the game I need.' Maybe that experience was a blessing, although I don't know if losing the British Open is ever a blessing."

Cruel Rules

Craig Stadler finally gets his revenge on the tree that cost him $37,000 in lost prize money. All it takes is a chain saw—and, he adds, "a little anger and an attitude."

THE CRYING TOWEL

Craig Stadler
1987 Andy Williams Open

Craig Stadler was battling for the lead in the third round of the 1987 Andy Williams Open (now called the Buick Invitational) at Torrey Pines Golf Course in La Jolla, California.

But then he ran into a little trouble on the fourteenth hole of the South Course. His wayward tee shot landed beneath a Leland cypress tree in a muddy lie on the right edge of the fairway. Because of low-hanging branches, the only way to play the shot was from an awkward kneeling position.

"I had one thought in mind," the Walrus recalled. "It was muddy and damp out there, and I had on light-colored trousers." Although he's never been mistaken for a *Gentlemen's Quarterly* cover boy, Stadler didn't want to finish the round in polyesters with unsightly knee stains.

So he placed a towel on the wet ground, knelt on it, and made his shot. Craig didn't think anything more about it and finished the round among the leaders.

The next day, the towel incident was replayed by NBC, which was broadcasting the final round. Immediately, astute golf fans lit up the tournament switchboard, claiming that Stadler had violated Rule 13–3 by illegally building a stance.

Once they were alerted, PGA officials studied *Decisions on the Rules of Golf* by the USGA and the Royal & Ancient Golf Club of St. Andrews. They determined that the use of the towel constituted an illegal improvement of the golfer's stance, which called for a two-stroke penalty.

Meanwhile, unaware of what was happening back in the clubhouse, Craig continued to play steady golf. He finished the tournament tied for second with J. C. Snead and Bobby Wadkins at 270, four strokes behind winner George Burns. Feeling pleased with himself, Stadler was strolling off the eighteenth green and calculating the amount of money he'd won when PGA Tour official Glenn Tait approached him with the bad news.

When Tait told him of the infraction, Craig grudgingly accepted the ruling. He figured that the two-stroke penalty would drop him a notch or two in the tournament standings and cost him a few thousand dollars in winnings.

Then Tait told him the really bad news.

Since neither Stadler nor his playing partners realized he had broken any rule at the time he used the towel, he hadn't penalized himself the two strokes. Consequently, he'd turned in an incorrect scorecard—an infraction that calls for disqualification. No matter that the offense had happened twenty-four hours earlier; the PGA DQ'd Stadler.

Craig had saved an eight-dollar laundry bill but wound up getting taken to the cleaners anyhow. Had he not been disqualified, Stadler would have earned $37,333.33. Now he had nothing to show for his four days of golf except a dirty towel.

At first, Stadler couldn't believe the ruling. He and Tait phoned P. J. Boatwright, the rules expert at the USGA. Boatwright said there was nothing that could be done.

"I thought about protesting," Stadler told reporters after the stunning development. "The rule book definition of a stance refers to a player 'placing his feet,' and my feet weren't on the towel. But the situation seemed hopeless. Neither of my playing partners said anything about it at the time. There must have been a hundred people standing around the tree, and nobody said anything. It's unfortunate. If somebody knew it [the rule], I wish they would have said something.

"It was in the rules. I just wish I knew about it. It's very disappointing, but what can I say? I broke a rule, I paid the price, and I just have to put it behind me.

"I didn't read the book on the decisions last year, and I didn't read the rule book this year. One of these days, I'm going to take a month off and read them both."

Later, after Craig had time to reflect on his ignoble incident, he said, "I still reckon a two-stroke penalty might have been a more fitting punishment for this insidious crime, but I tried to forget about the whole thing, and I think I handled myself pretty well when interviewed on television.

"It was very gratifying to discover that almost everyone who participated in a call-in vote arranged by ABC–TV felt that I'd been given a raw deal. My wife, Sue, reminded me that I would only play worse the more I wrenched over it, and she was right."

As much as Stadler wanted to forget about Towelgate, the incident triggered a storm of controversy over television's role in sports.

NBC golf analyst Bob Goalby said that TV viewers phoning the PGA to report undetected infractions during a tournament is akin to "fans calling the first-base umpire to complain. You just don't do that."

Added NBC executive producer Michael Weisman, "Technology is supposed to improve sport. But right now, technology is ruining sport."

Put another way, said Rick Reilly of *Sports Illustrated,* "The Big Eye is supposed to be bringing us the thrill of victory and the agony of defeat, not causing it." He added, "Once again television had gone beyond its old job as presenter of sports to alterer of them. Something's got to give, and so far, it has been sanity.

"And there should be some sort of statute of limitations. Stadler got jobbed because at some point—whether it was when his scorecard was approved or he was popping open his first beer of the evening—the round should have been declared over."

NBC's Andy Rosenberg, who directed the telecast, wondered if it was fair that Stadler was caught by TV when players finishing before the telecast escaped the electronic eye. "Our jobs are not to be tattletales or rules officials," he said. "Our job is to televise."

Boatwright, however, claimed that "the committee in charge has an obligation to follow up any information it gets and can apply it as long as the tournament is going on."

Golfer Lon Hinkle, who was with Stadler when the incident occurred, said he approved of the use of TV replays to spot violations. "I think it's good for the game," he declared. "It will make other golfers aware of the rules."

Arnold Palmer also agreed with the decision. "Craig happens to be a friend, but I'm certainly one who believes if an infraction is found, you have to do what they did," he told reporters at the time. "It's very unfortunate it happened. But it happens to all of us from time to time."

The cypress tree itself was sort of an outlaw. Years earlier, a USGA rule was passed to forbid the use of "mechanical aids" such as 150-yard stakes or marked sprinklers to help golfers measure yardage. Torrey Pines regulars asked then city golf superintendent Don Makie to figure out a legal way to give them yardage markers. So he planted thirty-six Leland cypresses—including the infamous tree that became the 150-yard marker on the fourteenth . . . and, later, Stadler's nemesis.

Craig tried to put the incident out of his mind, but reporters kept bringing up the subject every year when he arrived for the Torrey Pines tourney. Finally, in 1994, the Walrus growled, "Isn't the statute of limitations on this up yet? I don't want to talk about it anymore."

Meanwhile, the offending tree became a victim of karma. After having made Stadler a poor sap, it got sick from a fungus disease. It was trimmed several times in an effort to extend its life, but its health continued to deteriorate.

In 1995, Tom Wilson, a member of the tournament organizing committee, heard that the cypress was dying and needed to be cut down. He conjured up a great idea that he thought would appeal to Stadler.

"Craig," he asked, "how would you like to take a chain saw to that tree?"

Lighting up as if he had just drilled an ace, Stadler replied, "I'd love to turn that tree into kindling. There've been a few expletives deleted every time I've walked by it."

With reporters and photographers recording his moment of revenge, Craig cranked up the chain saw and attacked the tree. Soon the thirty-three-year-old cypress had been reduced to firewood. Fifteen plaque-sized pieces were shipped to Stadler's home in suburban Denver, where they were later auctioned off for charity.

"It felt great taking the chain saw to that tree," Craig recalled. "I didn't have to train for it. It didn't take much effort—just a little bit of anger and an attitude."

In professional golf, players who do not verse themselves in the rules do so at their own peril, as Craig Stadler can testify. In 1997, such ignorance cost Davis Love III nearly $100,000.

It's reasonable to assume that anyone who earns a living as a pro golfer would make it his or her business to be an expert on the *Rules of Golf*. But according to the USGA, in 1997 only one player from the LPGA Tour, PGA Tour, or Senior PGA Tour—the LPGA's Annika Sorenstam—bothered to attend one of thirteen rules workshops the organization conducted.

Davis, who is a member of the Tour's policy board, could have benefited from such a workshop.

He was gunning for a top-five finish at the Players Championship at Ponte Vedra Beach, Florida, when he lined up a putt on the par-three seventeenth green in the final round. While attempting a four-foot birdie putt, he took a practice stroke and accidentally brushed his ball with the toe of his putter. The ball moved about a foot. Knowing he had committed an infraction, Love winced and marked his ball at the new spot. He then set the ball down at the new spot and two-putted. He assessed himself a one-stroke penalty and marked a bogey four on his scorecard.

Under Rule 18–2, however, Love should have moved the ball back to its original position and taken a penalty stroke. By failing to replace his ball correctly, Love incurred the general penalty of two strokes for breach of Rule 18, which deals with playing the ball from an incorrect spot. He should have given himself a double-bogey five.

In the scorer's tent, he signed for a seventy-three rather than a seventy-four. Moments later, officials informed him that he had been disqualified for signing an incorrect scorecard. Only then did he learn of his error.

"I didn't know the rule," Love confessed later. "Obviously, if I had, I wouldn't have been disqualified."

It was an extremely expensive lesson. If he had returned the ball to its correct spot and made a bogey, Love would have finished at four-under 284 and in a four-way tie for seventh. That would have been worth $105,437 and twenty-five Ryder Cup points. If he had taken two penalty strokes and signed for a double-bogey five, Love would have finished at three-under 285 and in a five-way tie for tenth. That would have netted him $80,500 and two Ryder Cup points.

Instead, Love headed home with only about $6,500 in earnings—the equivalent of last-place money.

"WHAT A STUPID I AM"

Roberto De Vicenzo
1968 Masters

April 14, 1968, is a date that will forever live in golfing infamy. It's the day when Roberto De Vicenzo lost a chance to win the Masters because of a slip of the pen. And it wasn't even his pen.

Roberto's playing partner, Tommy Aaron, had accidentally marked down the wrong score on De Vicenzo's scorecard—an error that went undetected until it was too late. Roberto was disqualified. Instead of preparing for a play-off the next day, he was watching Bob Goalby don the green jacket.

De Vicenzo had arrived at Augusta National with high hopes, gunning for his second major title in two years. In 1967, at his twelfth appearance at the British Open, he captured the crown with a 278, two strokes better than runner-up Jack Nicklaus.

The amiable, stoop-shouldered, balding Argentine was a crowd favorite. He had joined the pro circuit at the age of fifteen and began making friends and winning prize money throughout the world. Fans loved his self-effacing humor, broken English, and even his reputation for erratic play—brilliant one week, dreadful the next.

At the 1968 Masters, De Vicenzo stayed among the leaders by firing rounds of sixty-nine, seventy-three, and seventy. Going into the final round, he was only two shots from pace setter Gary Player and one stroke behind five others, including Goalby.

Before his 1 P.M. tee time, Roberto went out to the practice tee and worked on his swing. He returned to the locker room, changed his sweat-soaked shirt, and guzzled ice water. Talking to a reporter, De Vicenzo said that since it was his forty-fifth birthday, he hoped that Lady Luck would have a present for him on the course.

She wasted no time, giving him a gift on the four-hundred-yard, par-four first hole. After walloping his drive straight down the fairway, Roberto hit a nine iron. The ball cleared the lip of a bunker on the left front, bounced once, and rolled into the cup for a remarkable eagle. With one amazing shot, De Vicenzo had vaulted into a first-place tie.

As he walked up to the green to retrieve his ball from the cup, the

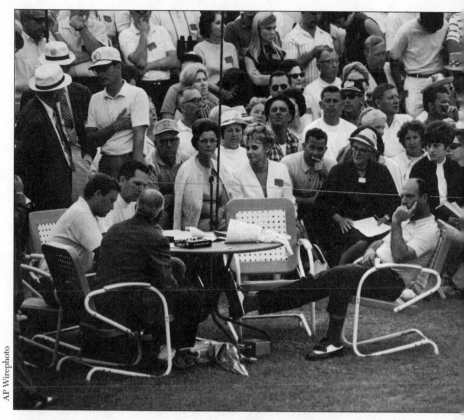

Roberto De Vicenzo (right) sits glumly at the officials' table as he hears the shocking news that he has been disqualified for turning in the wrong score.

cheering crowd spontaneously broke into a full chorus of "Happy Birthday to You," much to his delight.

Sensing he could really win the Masters, Roberto birdied the second and third holes. With each hole he played, the size of his gallery increased and he fed off the spectators' enthusiasm. Fans shouted, "Come on, D-V!" and "Way to go, Roberto!"

De Vicenzo made the turn in thirty-one and had a one-stroke lead over Goalby, who, while playing two groups behind him, had made three birdies on the front nine.

Rather than play conservatively, Roberto attacked the course. On eleven, he went for the pin, ignoring the water on the left, and hit a great shot within four feet of the hole, only to blow the birdie putt. His tee shot on the par-three twelfth, over the creek, landed within twelve feet of the hole. He made that putt for a birdie.

Two more pars, a birdie on the fifteenth, and another par left him at seven under for the day as he stepped to the seventeenth tee. Meanwhile, Goalby—whose highest previous Masters finish was twenty-fifth—surprised everyone. He broke out of a second-place traffic jam with birdies at the thirteenth and fourteenth. On the 520-yard, par-five fifteenth, he blasted a three iron that carried the pond and rolled dead eight feet from the pin. He knocked it in for an eagle to go one stroke up on Roberto.

But on the four-hundred-yard, par-four seventeenth, De Vicenzo answered the challenge. He hit a pitching wedge to within three feet of the hole and drained it for a birdie that put him back in a tie. The hundreds of spectators around the green saw him make three; so did the millions of viewers glued to their TV sets.

Naturally, his partner, Tommy Aaron, witnessed the birdie. But, inexplicably, Aaron marked down four on Roberto's scorecard.

On the final hole, Roberto felt the suffocating pressure. After pulling his approach to the left, he putted the ball over a mound to within five feet of the cup. But then he watched aghast as his par putt hit the edge of the rim and spun out.

Grimacing as if he had been shot in the chest, Roberto tapped in for a bogey and walked slowly off the green, oblivious to the tremendous ovation he was receiving from the gallery. Because of the bogey, he had toppled into second place. The tournament was Goalby's to win. He needed to par the final three holes to claim the championship.

Still wincing over his blown putt, the disappointed Argentine walked over to the scorer's table. When Aaron handed him the scorecard, Roberto gave a hasty glance and signed it. In past tournaments, De Vicenzo always took time to go over the numbers on his card to make sure they were accurate. But a network TV producer urged him to come quickly to the interview room.

Back on the course, Goalby parred the sixteenth hole. But on seventeen, he left his approach far short of the pin and three-putted for a bogey, which dropped him into a tie with Roberto. Angry with himself, Goalby sliced his drive on the final hole. But he recovered nicely to par it.

Everyone assumed there would be a play-off the next day. But that wasn't to be. The real action was now happening in the scorer's tent.

Moments after De Vicenzo was whisked away for his interview, Aaron realized he had incorrectly jotted a four instead of a three for Roberto on the seventeenth. Further compounding the error, he wrote down a nine-hole total of thirty-five instead of thirty-four and an eighteen-hole total of sixty-six instead of sixty-five.

Aaron pointed out the mistake to one of the committeemen, who then checked De Vicenzo's card and referred the matter to members of the rules committee. According to *Rules of Golf*, Rule 38, Paragraph 3, "No alteration may be made on a card after the competitor has returned it to the Committee. If the competitor returns a score for any hole lower than actually played, he shall be disqualified. A score higher than actually played must stand as returned." That meant De Vicenzo's erroneous score of sixty-six would have to stand, even though he had really shot sixty-five.

The rules committee took the card to Bobby Jones, founder of the Masters, who was in his cottage watching the tournament on television. Jones asked if there was any way to interpret the rules differently so that Roberto could be in a play-off with Goalby. But there was none. The rule was there, and the rule was followed.

De Vicenzo was called into the scorer's tent and given the appalling news: Because of the sixty-six on the scorecard, he finished with an official four-round total of 278, one stroke behind the 277 shot by Bob Goalby, who was now the new Masters champion.

Once the shock wore off, Roberto returned to the interview room, where he said, "I just signed the wrong card. The other fellow [Aaron] put down a four. It's my fault."

Goalby won $20,000, while De Vicenzo pocketed $15,000 for his second-place finish. But he lost out on any chance to collect an estimated $1 million that went to the winner in promotional fees.

At the presentation ceremony, tournament chairman Clifford Roberts told De Vicenzo, "I and Bobby Jones want you to know that we would love to declare two winners this year. If ever a tournament had two great champions, we have got them here."

An hour later, Roberto and Goalby met the entire press corps, who gave De Vicenzo a rousing ovation. Looking drawn and tired, and with an interpreter beside him explaining some of the questions in Spanish, he answered all queries with grace and humor.

In his fractured English, he said, "I made the wrong score. I feel so sorry for myself. What a stupid I am."

De Vicenzo didn't alibi or blame anyone but himself for the scorecard error. He declined to criticize Aaron, but said, "Tommy feels like I feel—very bad. I think the rule is hard."

When asked what might have happened in Argentina under such conditions, Roberto smiled and remarked, "We play friendly golf there.

"But I congratulate Bob Goalby, he gave me so much pressure that I lose my brains."

Said Goalby, "I'd be a liar if I didn't say I was happy to win. But I regret the way I had to win. I wish it would have been in a play-off tomorrow."

So did many golf fans. Golf officials were deluged with telephone calls, letters, and telegrams—almost all critical. Many offered suggestions, and all expressed regret that such a thing could happen.

Golf writers and golfers took sides on whether the rule made sense.

One writer sarcastically noted that Goalby was the Masters champion because he "proved he was a better bookkeeper than Roberto De Vicenzo."

New York Times columnist Arthur Daley claimed the rule was outdated. "Golf is the only sport that obliges each contestant to be his own scorekeeper . . . It no longer belongs in major championships where milling thousands of fans charge all over the course and where television magnifies the impact of the event and where huge purses add to the emotional pressure. Furthermore, no other phase of athletic activity demands more intense concentration on the business at hand than golf. No player should be required to risk distraction by also serving as a bookkeeper."

Said *Time* magazine, "Certainly nobody in his right mind gives himself a higher score for a hole than he actually shot. Why should he be penalized at all for such an obviously unintentional goof?"

But De Vicenzo's fellow golfers defended the rule and laid the blame at his feet. "It was a foolish blunder," said Tony Jacklin. Added Lee Trevino, "A player should be responsible for his own score. Roberto goofed—and had to pay."

Even today, the controversy still simmers. In a 1997 column in *Golf World*, John Huggan claimed that Goalby had an opportunity to be a golfing legend if he had refused to accept the green jacket.

"Think about it," wrote Huggan. "Apart from the fact that such an action is entirely the right thing to do, Goalby was in a no-lose position. By insisting on a play-off he would have been twenty-four hours away from being either the new Masters champion or the sportsman of the century. Or both. Also, what could the officials have done? Disqualify him for not wearing his jacket?"

Today, Goalby insists he did the only thing possible. "The *Rules of Golf* didn't allow me to refuse the win," he said. "That never occurred to me. Roberto signing for the wrong score is no different than if a guy hits out of bounds. It just happened to be at the Masters, and it just happened to be on television. Besides, I really didn't give a damn. It was his problem."

Goalby is the only Masters winner whose green jacket is stained by an errant pen. More people remember who lost that tournament than who won it. "I have never been given credit for winning, and I shot one of the lowest scores ever," Goalby pointed out. At the time, his (and Roberto's) 277 was the fourth lowest in Masters history.

De Vicenzo bounced back from his calamity three weeks later to win the Houston Champions, his last PGA Tour victory. He won more than one hundred international titles among his 230 career victories. Inducted into the PGA Hall of Fame in 1979 and the World Golf Hall of Fame in 1989, Roberto reflected on that ignominious day. "It's not so bad. I think more people know me because I *didn't* win the Masters than if I did win it. I had offers to play all over the world. I became famous."

As for Tommy Aaron, he's had to live with the guilt of wrecking De Vicenzo's chance at a Masters title. The day after the tournament, the morning dew on the course hadn't even dried when Tommy became the butt of a new joke:

"What's the free drink some bars serve after you've paid for three?"

"I don't know. What?"

"A Tommy Aaron—because it's the fourth shot you didn't ask for."

Jackie Pung
1957 U.S. Women's Open

The 1968 Masters wasn't professional golf's first major decided by a scorecard error. That dishonor went to the 1957 U.S. Women's Open.

When Jackie Pung triumphantly walked off the eighteenth green at Winged Foot Golf Club, everyone believed she was the Open champion. Friends and family embraced the jovial Hawaiian-born housewife. Reporters surrounded her and peppered her with questions.

But moments later her tears of joy turned into a cascade of anguish.

While fans hailed her as the new Women's Open queen, Jackie received the terrible, shocking news that she had been disqualified for signing an erroneous scorecard. The title—and the $1,800 first prize—instead went to Betsy Rawls, who carded the second-best score of 299, one higher than Pung's total.

Officials had discovered that Betty Jameson, Jackie's playing partner and marker, had written a five on Pung's scorecard for the fourth hole when, in fact, Jackie had scored a six. But the eighteen-hole total was correct on the scorecard. In her excitement about winning, Pung didn't notice the mistake. She saw that her total score was accurate, so she signed her card.

But the rigid and inflexible rules of golf were clear: If a competitor turns in a score for any hole lower than actually played, she shall be disqualified. So tournament officials DQ'd Jackie.

Incredibly, Jameson was disqualified at the same time—because of a scorecard error Pung made! Jackie, who was Betty's marker, had mistakenly put down a five on Betty's scorecard for the same fourth hole after Betty had shot a six. The only difference in the penalty was the consequence—Jameson was not in contention, having shot an eighty-five in the final round.

The awards ceremony was almost too much for Pung to bear. As the trophy was handed to Rawls, a few feet away, a shattered Jackie stared in bitter disappointment.

"It was an awful mistake," admitted Pung, her eyes bloodshot and her voice hoarse from crying. "It is due to a great deal of excitement. Both Betty and I knew we had sixes. My mistake and Betty's was in not repeating to each other what we had at that hole and seeing it was on the card.

"I'm heartbroken. I thought I won this tournament. It meant a lot to me and my family. I would've won $1,800 and a bonus from a manufacturing company I represent. Now I have absolutely nothing to show for playing here this week."

Members of Winged Foot felt so sorry for Jackie that they raised $3,000 to help ease the pain of losing out of the first-place prize money. But the salve couldn't quite soothe the wound.

Pung never came close to winning a major again.

John Kelly

After his club catches in the grass for an instant, T. C. Chen inadvertently hits the ball a second time. This photo captures the precise moment of the infamous double-hit.

THE DOUBLE-HIT

T. C. Chen
1985 U.S. Open

Golf historians like to say that nobody wins the U.S. Open, somebody loses it. Unfortunately for T. C. Chen, he lost it—on a shot never before seen in a major.

Actually, it was two shots—but on the same swing!

The infraction did more than cost Chen a one-stroke penalty. It repelled his charge toward the championship.

A second-year pro on the PGA Tour, the twenty-seven-year-old Taiwanese was playing his first Open in 1985 at Oakland Hills Country Club near Detroit. No one ever considered Chen a contender—until he opened everyone's eyes with the rarest of all golf shots, the double eagle.

It happened in the first round on the 527-yard, par-five second hole, a slight dogleg left. Chen drove between the bunkers that pinched the fairway and was left with 240 yards to the front of the green, which was guarded by four small bunkers. Chen then blasted a three wood that flew straight at the flagstick, hit the fringe, and ran fifty-five feet right into the cup for an astounding two.

Because nearly the entire gallery was elsewhere, only about twenty people saw the ball roll into the hole. They raised so feeble a cry that Chen wasn't even aware he had holed the shot until he walked up to the green, where a scoreboard attendant give him the good news.

"This is a story," T. C. recalled at the end of the day. "When I hit the ball, it went straight to the pin. I didn't know it went into the hole until I walked onto the green, even though I heard a yell after I hit the ball. I feel great and so surprised."

It was the first double eagle in the eighty-five-year history of the Open.

The two inspired Chen to fire a round of sixty-five, which equaled the competitive course record and gave him a one-stroke lead over Fred Couples.

The next day, Chen was sporting a white cap on which the national flag of Taiwan was sewn. The miniature flag had been shipped to Chen by a representative of the Taiwan delegation in Washington, D.C. Suddenly, the five-foot, ten-inch, 140-pound T. C. (short for Tze-Chung) was the crowd favorite. Playing before a large and enthusiastic gallery, Chen shot sixty-nine in the second round to maintain a slim one-stroke lead over Jay Haas and Andy North. Chen's 134 tied the lowest score for the first thirty-six holes of an Open, set by Jack Nicklaus when he won the Open at Baltusrol in 1980.

Everyone was taking T. C. seriously when, in the third round, he shot his second straight sixty-nine. He had matched an Open record of 203 for fifty-four holes (set by George Burns in 1981 at Merion) and held a two-stroke lead over North.

Chen, the son of a golf course superintendent in Taipei, had become an overnight star. He was the lead story in sports pages across America—and on the front pages in Taiwan. He had made believers out of his fellow pros.

"He doesn't seem to be nervous at all," said Johnny Miller, who won the Open in 1973. "When you play in the Open, you've got to keep a grip on your emotions."

Miller's words proved profound the next day.

The final round was played in a steady rain that soaked the golfers and gallery but left the course playable. After the first two holes, Chen had doubled his lead over North to four strokes. They both parred the next two holes. As they moved to the fifth tee, it looked like T. C.—now eight under—was not going to give anyone a chance to catch up. Although he had never won a PGA Tour event, T. C. had had victories in the Japanese Open and the Korean Open during the previous two months. Confidence surged through his veins.

Chen split the fairway with his drive on the 457-yard, par-four fifth hole. He showed no signs of wavering or of falling victim to nerves. That's what made the next shot so mystifying. He pulled out his four iron and looked at the pin 175 yards away. It was set in the right front of the green behind a bunker.

As he surveyed the situation, T. C. turned to his caddie, Mike Lealos, who gave a disapproving look. "You don't like the four iron?" Chen asked.

"I like the five iron."

Chen shook his head and said, "I don't want to hook it. Trees too close. I want to cut it."

As he tried to cut the shot from left to right to avoid the trees, T. C. pushed his ball at least fifty yards off line, wide of the green and into heavy rough among a stand of big trees. Even though he was in the woods, Chen still had a clear shot to the green. He wanted to land the ball on the edge of the green by hitting between two large tree trunks. But in trying to play close to the hole, he misjudged his shot. His poorly executed sand-wedge pitch left the ball short in clumpy, wet, tall grass about twenty yards from the green.

Then came the most astonishing swing in U.S. Open history. Taking his wedge, Chen chopped down on the ball. It popped almost straight up and seemed to hang in midair. His follow-through was delayed a split second by the thick grass. When the club broke through the grass, it hit the still suspended ball again! The wedge flipped the ball high and to the left, where it landed twenty feet away from him onto the fringe of the green.

Chen stood frozen in shock, his face pale and blank. He had never seen a double-hit before—let alone made one. And of all of the times for it to happen, he had to make this fluke swing in the final round of the U.S. Open.

According to the *Rules of Golf,* "If a player's club strikes the ball more than once in the course of a stroke, the player shall count the stroke and add a penalty stroke, making two strokes in all."

Even though Chen had swung only four times, he lay in five, not four. He was so shaken by his stunning double flub that he sent his chip eight feet past the hole and took two putts to get down. He had made a quadruple-bogey eight. His four-stroke margin had been wiped out, leaving him tied for the lead with North.

"Now I know," Chen muttered to his caddie, "I should have hit the five iron to the center of the green."

The more T. C. thought about the five iron he should have hit and the wedge that he double-hit, the more his concentration wandered on the course.

Chen bogeyed each of the next three holes. Within four holes, he had gone from four strokes ahead to three strokes behind. The shell-shocked golfer never recovered and finished the round with a shaky seventy-seven, tying for second place at par 280. Had it not been for that blasted double-hit, he would have tied winner Andy North, who shot a one-under 279, and forced a play-off.

In the locker room afterward, Chen relived the awful moment that cost him the victory. "I opened the face [of the club] and hit the ball soft to make the ball spin, but then I double-hit it. I never had hit a double before. It upset me a lot. It stayed on my mind. I had a stupid game today, but I can only blame me. Bad head."

In his disappointment, T. C. thoughtfully turned to his caddie and apologized for losing the Open. "He told me 'Sorry,'" Mike Lealos recalled. "He told me 'Sorry' two or three times."

Denis Watson
1985 U.S. Open

The penalty on T. C. Chen's double-hit wasn't the only bizarre infraction at the 1985 U.S. Open.

Denis Watson was slapped with a two-stroke penalty because he failed to hit a ball in time. And, as it did Chen, the violation cost Watson a crack at winning the title.

In the first round, Watson faced a twenty-foot putt for par on the eighth hole. The South African knocked the ball on a perfect line, but it died at the lip of the cup and tantalizingly hung over the edge. The ball was so close to falling that Watson felt it had a good chance of dropping.

Believing good things happen to those who wait, Denis stood near the cup for over forty seconds. His patience paid off. The ball plopped into the hole, and Watson broke out in a big grin. His marker jotted down a par four on the scorecard.

Patience can be a virtue, but in golf it can also be an infraction. As Watson worked his way through the crowd, he was stopped at the ninth tee by Montford Johnson, a member of the USGA executive committee who was serving on the rules committee for the Open.

Johnson had the unpleasant task of informing Denis that the golfer had violated Rule 16-1h of the *Rules of Golf,* which allows a golfer "enough time to reach the hole without undue delay and an additional ten seconds to determine whether the ball is at rest. If by then the ball has not fallen into the hole, it is deemed to be at rest."

Johnson said that Watson had taken an undue amount of time and therefore would be assessed a two-stroke penalty. Watson's par had turned into a double-bogey six. Denis gritted his teeth and played on, finishing the round at two-over seventy-two.

Watson put the infraction out of his mind. And it would have been forgotten by everyone—if he hadn't played so well over the next three rounds. He stayed close to the leaders and finished with a total of even-par 280.

Much to his chagrin, his score turned out to be only one stroke higher than winner Andy North's 279. Denis had finished in a tie for second with none other than T. C. Chen.

Watson couldn't help but look back at his costly first-round two-shot penalty. Had he tapped in the ball on the eighth hole before the time limit was up, he would have scored a five and finished the tournament at 279, forcing a play-off with North.

"I never gave a thought to that penalty once it happened," said Watson later. "It was over with, and there was nothing I could do about it."

Asked what he thought of the time limit, he replied, "The ten-second rule is cranky."